DAILY COMPANION
FOR
MARRIED COUPLES

"Abide in my love."—Jn 15:9

DAILY COMPANION
FOR
MARRIED COUPLES

**MINUTE MEDITATIONS FOR EVERY DAY
CONTAINING A SCRIPTURE QUOTE OR
INSPIRATIONAL READING,
A REFLECTION, AND A PRAYER**

By
Allan F. Wright

Illustrated

CATHOLIC BOOK PUBLISHING CORP.
New Jersey

CONTENTS

NIHIL OBSTAT: Fr. Philip-Michael F. Tangorra, S.T.L.
Censor Librorum

IMPRIMATUR: ✠ Most Rev. Arthur J. Serratelli, S.T.D., S.S.L., D.D.
Bishop of Paterson

January 3, 2016

The Nihil Obstat and Imprimatur are official declarations that a book or a pamphlet is free of doctrinal or moral error. No implication is contained therein that those who have granted the Nihil Obstat and Imprimatur agree with the contents, opinions or statements expressed.

Scripture quotations (unless otherwise noted) are taken from the ST. JOSEPH NEW CATHOLIC BIBLE® Copyright © 2019 by Catholic Book Publishing Corp. Used with permission. All rights reserved.

(T-191)

ISBN 978-1-941243-50-3

© 2016 Catholic Book Publishing Corp., N.J.
Printed in China   21 HA 3
catholicbookpublishing.com

They say that love is blind but marriage restores the vision. While there is both humor and truth to that saying, Catholics take a view of the sanctity of the sacrament of marriage quite seriously. For Catholics, the sacrament of marriage is one of the deepest signs of God's love. The union of man and woman in Holy Matrimony speak the language of the self-giving love of the Holy Trinity. In the grandeur and beauty of the union of spouses in marriage, symbolized by their physical union which leads in a mysterious way to the creation of a new human person, we recognize God's plan for man and woman in marriage.

It's true today as it was hundreds of years ago that a person truly in love wants to be bound forever to their beloved which is precisely the gift that marriage provides. The Catholic Church is truly a defender of the beauty, goodness, and truth of God's design of marriage articulated through natural law and through the word of God. While there is no perfect marriage, we all desire a healthy marriage where, come what may, we are assured of God's presence on the journey and our spouse's support each step of the way.

The Scripture quotes, passages from Church documents, and thoughts from the Saints which begin most days in this book are there to help give us direction in living the vocation of married life to the fullest. The other quotes are from friends who inspire us by their personal faith and joy and still others who bear witness to the beauty of married life through their commitment to love as God loves.

A great debt of gratitude goes, of course, to my wife Desiree, who is a constant source of love, forgiveness, and faith as we go through this life helping each other get to Heaven. The best gift we can give our four children is our love for God and for one another. It's my hope that these reflections may be a source of comfort and guidance, and may even challenge you to grow closer to Jesus together.

Allan F. Wright

ELIGHT yourself in the Lord, and he will give you what your heart desires.

JAN. **1**

—Ps 37:4

With this ring...

REFLECTION. It's nice to dream about winning the lottery or making our first million. As we mature we realize that we were made for more. The best gifts can be found not in things but in relationships.

Pray for your spouse every day and thank God that you found your heart's desire in them.

PRAYER. *Mary, Mother of Jesus, pray for us and bring your Son our needs as you did at Cana.*

 N THE third day there was a wedding at Cana in Galilee. The mother of Jesus was there.

JAN. **2**

—Jn 2:1

Let's get this party started

REFLECTION. Jesus' first miracle was performed at the wedding at Cana where He turned water into wine. This beautiful and miraculous act saved the bride and groom and their families from shame.

Where Jesus is present the party continues! He desires that our joy be complete.

PRAYER. *Jesus, fill our marriage with joy and laughter; let our cups overflow!*

HEY say that it is not worth making a lifelong commitment because we do not know what tomorrow will bring. I ask you, instead, to be revolutionaries.
—Pope Francis

JAN. 3

Making a definitive decision

REFLECTION. Marriage involves a lifelong commitment because in the Catholic understanding, marriage is a covenant. It is more than a covenant between a husband and wife for God is at the very heart of their love.

With God at the center of marriage we can give a wholehearted yes to this journey.

PRAYER. *God, be at the heart of our marriage. May we love each other as You love us.*

BOVE all, love each other deeply, because love covers a multitude of sins.
—1 Pet 4:8

JAN. 4

Love is the measure

REFLECTION. In marriage there will be daily inconveniences and misunderstandings that couples will have to deal with because no one is perfect.

Pride puts "self" first and leads to division and pain. Love, on the other hand, puts the other first and forgives and heals those wounds.

PRAYER. *Jesus, let my love for my spouse be authentic.*

8

TRUST in the Lord with all your heart, and do not lean on your own understanding. In all your ways acknowledge him, and he will make straight your paths. —Prov 3:5-6

JAN.
5

Trust God in all things

REFLECTION. It's an illusion to think we can control all situations. Even the best laid strategic plans can seemingly fail.

God desires the best for your marriage so be sure to include God in your plans by praying for and with one another each day, and He will make your path straight.

PRAYER. *Come Holy Spirit, guide us through our lives together and bless our marriage.*

———————

 BE STRONG and courageous; do not be frightened or dismayed, for the Lord your God is with you wherever you go. —Jos 1:9

JAN.
6

We can get through this together

REFLECTION. Marriage is the joyful union of husband and wife which brings many blessings and challenges along the way.

When there are difficult times remember that you are not alone; God is with you and He promises to be with you for better or worse.

PRAYER. *Thank You, Lord, for the joys and blessings in our lives. Stand with us as we stand together.*

AUTHENTIC married love is caught up into divine love.

JAN.
7

—*Gaudium et spes*

It was God's plan all along

REFLECTION. Marriage is not a human invention but rather has its origins in the heart of God the Father. How beautiful to be part of His plan.

We are called to love as God loves and to give our lives to each other through marriage. Remember that your marriage is a sacrament, an outward sign of God's love.

PRAYER. *God, the author of marriage, assist us in living and loving as You desire.*

 THE sacrament of Matrimony signifies the union of Christ and the Church.

JAN.
8

—*St. Joseph Guide to the Catechism*

How did Christ love the Church?

REFLECTION. St. Paul knew intimately the story of Jesus and His sacrificial death on the Cross. This is the model for a man in loving his wife—giving one's whole being for the other.

This is not easy in practice, but in trying we become like Christ which is the goal of every Catholic.

PRAYER. *Jesus, may we be examples of selfless love in how we treat each other.*

HE child grew and became strong, filled with wisdom, and the favor of God was upon him. —Lk 2:40

JAN.
9

Jesus grew up in a family

REFLECTION. Jesus is the Son of God and the child of Mary and Joseph. It was God's will that Jesus have His parents guide and love Him.

Be open to life and the blessing of children. God's favor is with you as well and together your child will be strong and filled with wisdom.

PRAYER. *Holy Spirit, bless us with children and give us wisdom to guide them each step they take.*

———————

HE grace of Matrimony is intended to perfect the couple's love and to strengthen their indissoluble unity.
—*St. Joseph Guide to the Catechism*

JAN.
10

In giving we live

REFLECTION. In marriage we no longer live for ourselves. This experience is eye-opening for most people after the honeymoon period ends.

It is the beginning of new life however where authentic love can blossom in new and beautiful ways. It's true, when we die to self we can begin to live as God intended in love.

PRAYER. *Heavenly Father, let us draw close to You and model true love to our spouse.*

I F I speak in the tongues of men and of angels, but have not love, I am nothing more than a noisy gong or a clanging cymbal.

JAN.
11

—1 Cor 13:1

Noise annoys

REFLECTION. Corinth was the brass-making capital of the ancient world. Imagine the noise and banging as the artisans worked at their craft.

Without love in our words and actions we are not much different than those artisans. Let us do all things with love and rise above the "noise" which deafens true love.

PRAYER. *Loving Father, may we lead with love as we grow together in faith.*

T HEN the man said: "This at last is bone of my bones and flesh of my flesh."

JAN.
12

—Gen 2:23

Creative differences

REFLECTION. Adam experienced original solitude. He longed to give himself to another, so God created a person like himself with some beautiful differences.

Rejoice in the gift of your spouse and even in your differences.

PRAYER. *Jesus, help us savor each other's differences and rejoice that we are not alone.*

MY dove,... let me see your face, let me hear your voice, for your voice is sweet, and your face is lovely.

JAN.
13

—Song 2:14

Love you more

REFLECTION. Love, like faith, is not solely an intellectual pursuit for it involves our whole being, emotions and all. Our desire for one another is a reflection of God's love for us so we should not be afraid to express our love and heartfelt desire for one another.

Make a point of expressing your love for each other each day.

PRAYER. *Gentle Father, increase our longing for one another at every stage of life.*

NE thing about married life is that you just never know what is around the corner. —Janie and Joseph Strummer

JAN.
14

Never a dull moment

REFLECTION. They say that if you want to make God laugh you should tell Him your plans. While God may not let us in on what's next in life, He reminds us that He is there through it all: the good, the bad and the ugly!

With God at the center of our lives we can get through anything.

PRAYER. *Loving Lord, increase our faith and sense of humor as we take what life gives us.*

WHAT are you looking for?
—Jn 1:38

A revealing question

REFLECTION. The first words from Jesus in St. John's Gospel are a question. What are you looking for? In marriage we realize that there is no "perfect" person but perhaps the person who is perfect for us.

Rejoice in the spouse you have made a vow to love and you will realize that they are what you are looking for.

PRAYER. *God of love, thank You for giving me my heart's desire in my spouse.*

BELOVED, since God loved us so much, we should love one another — 1 Jn 4:11

He loved us in our imperfection

REFLECTION. God loves all people. Not just the "holy" or the "saints" among us. As we try to model that love we know it can be difficult because marriages are made of imperfect people.

Let us try our best to allow God's love to move through us so we can love our imperfect spouse perfectly all the days of our life.

PRAYER. *Loving Father, if we confess our sins You are faithful and just to forgive us and cleanse us from all unrighteousness.*

14

LL things are lawful, but not all things are beneficial. —1 Cor 10:23

Do the right thing

REFLECTION. There are things which we do and fail to do which are not enforced by any laws. There are no laws per se enforcing housework. Yet hanging up clothes and putting away the clean dishes are all ways that we can show love to one another.

In marriage the number one law is the law of love.

PRAYER. *Lord God, let me model Jesus in love and remind me to take the initiative to serve.*

 AVE the courage "to swim against the tide" and also have the courage to be happy. —Pope Francis

Joyful minority

REFLECTION. The choice to marry is a bold one. More and more people choose a lifestyle other than traditional marriage within the context of a Mass.

Be joyful that your marriage is an outward sign of God's love, a public demonstration that God has a joy-filled plan for your marriage. Be as St. Paul recommends, the fragrance of Christ.

PRAYER. *Mary, Our Mother, guide and pray for us as we live our public witness of God's love.*

E CANNOT all do great things, but we can do small things with great love. —Blessed Mother Teresa

JAN. 19

Start today

REFLECTION. We may think of Mother Teresa as a major Saint of our times, and she is well known worldwide for her holiness.

When we look at her actions we find that she was always attentive to the person in her presence. Her smile, her touch, and her care were small things done with great love. Show that same love today.

PRAYER. *Jesus, open my eyes to those small things I can do to serve my spouse.*

 HE Eucharist is the Sacrament of Love; it signifies Love; it produces love. —Saint Thomas Aquinas

JAN. 20

Given for you

REFLECTION. Marriage is often celebrated in the context of Mass which is appropriate because what we celebrate in the Eucharist we live out in marriage.

We give our whole selves to the other in and through our body. Married people say to one another: this is my body given for you.

PRAYER. *Heavenly Father, thank You for the gift of Jesus and my spouse. May our love model Yours.*

VERY kingdom divided against itself is laid waste, and every city or household divided against itself cannot survive.

—Mt 12:25

JAN. **21**

United not divided

REFLECTION. Division is one of the greatest tools of the Devil. It usually starts with something small but can easily blossom into something bigger very quickly.

When arguments come, and they will, make sure to "nip it in the bud" before it gets out of hand, and never allow outside forces to divide what God has brought together.

PRAYER. *Loving Father, grant us the wisdom to handle small problems before they get out of control.*

 O NOT be afraid, then, when love makes demands. Do not be afraid when love requires sacrifice.

—Pope St. John Paul II

JAN. **22**

Opportunities for growth

REFLECTION. We tend to shy away from things that require sacrifice, yet we find that when we sacrifice we are better for it.

Your spouse is worth the sacrifice of your time, effort, and love especially when it's most difficult and inconvenient. This love lived in the home will be the model for your children.

PRAYER. *My Lord and God, thank You for modeling love and sacrifice in Jesus Christ.*

THE experience of evil, within and without, makes itself felt in the relationships between man and woman.

JAN.
23

—*St. Joseph Guide to the Catechism*

Overcome evil with good

REFLECTION. The fact that we are not perfect and are tempted to do the wrong thing is quite real. When we examine our hearts and the local news we are aware that evil exists and can easily impact our relationships.

Overcome evil with prayer for and with each other on a daily basis to protect yourself and to recognize evil.

PRAYER. *Merciful Father, draw close to us as we grow close to You.*

BY ITS very nature the institution of marriage and married love is ordered to the procreation and education of offspring.

JAN.
24

—*St. Joseph Guide to the Catechism*

Called to serve

REFLECTION. Years, months, weeks, and days go into the planning of the big wedding day. Some women's minds are filled with thoughts of this glorious day since their childhood.

As important as planning this day is, planning a life of service together will define your marriage for better or worse.

PRAYER. *Jesus, may we always be open to life and to serve those whom You bring our way.*

WILL betroth you to me in faithfulness. And you shall know the Lord. —Hos 2:22 **JAN. 25**

You are chosen

REFLECTION. One of the beautiful images God uses in speaking of our relationship to Him is marriage. What a wonderful way to describe the love God has for us. A total, free, and faithful gift of self to the other.

An unconditional love which desires the good of the other is the goal each and every day in marriage.

PRAYER. *Lord God, thank You for choosing us and always being faithful to us in love.*

 OVE takes up where knowledge leaves off. —St. Thomas Aquinas **JAN. 26**

Enter the mystery of love

REFLECTION. We can never know absolutely everything about our spouse. Even after years of marriage we hear older couples say, "I never knew that about you."

Nuptial love asks us to love the other even when they seem to be a mystery to us. Your spouse is not a puzzle to be solved but a mystery to be savored.

PRAYER. *Eternal Father, let me love my spouse even when I don't fully understand them.*

E DID what was right in the Lord's sight.
—2 Kgs 22:2

JAN.

27

Where ever, when ever

REFLECTION. Josiah was one of the good kings of Israel and did what the Lord commanded. How easy is it to think we know what's right and true without any guidance or counsel.

Through prayer, discernment, study of God's word and the teaching of God's Church we too can know what's right in the Lord's sight.

PRAYER. *God our Father, with You leading us we will do what's right in Your eyes.*

ORD, grant that I might not so much seek to be loved as to love.
—St. Francis of Assisi

JAN.

28

Love leads

REFLECTION. We all desire to love and be loved. St. Francis prayed for the grace to lead with love and the grace to be detached from the desire to be loved.

There will be times when our loving actions will be overlooked and our love unreturned even in marriage. At those times ask for the grace to continue to love and not count the cost.

PRAYER. *Holy Spirit, stir within me an ardent desire to love and not count the cost.*

F WE confess our sins, he who is faithful and just will forgive our sins. —1 Jn 1:9

JAN.
29

Imperfect people, perfect union

REFLECTION. Jesus knew that belief in Him as the Son of God would not make His followers instant Saints.

We all need to be forgiven and renewed by the sacrament of reconciliation. Frequent this sacrament often and let the forgiveness God extends to you overflow to your spouse.

PRAYER. *Merciful Father, let forgiveness be but one of our expressions of love.*

 OW important it is to have intergenerational exchanges and dialogues, especially within the context of the family. —Pope Francis

JAN.
30

Wisdom from parents and grandparents

REFLECTION. The older we get the wiser our parents and grandparents seem to be. While they may not be perfect, they do have some wisdom from the successes and failures they've experienced in life.

Go to them often to speak but most of all to ask good questions and then listen.

PRAYER. *Lord God, thank You for the gift of our parents and grandparents; protect and guide them.*

OW that the wall had been rebuilt, I had the doors set up and the gatekeepers...were put in charge of them

JAN.
31

—Neh 7:1

A proper defense

REFLECTION. Nehemiah rebuilt the walls of Jerusalem. Walls were an important defense for any city to protect it from those who wished to do harm.

Our marriages are often under attack by internal and external forces. Check with each other often so harmful forces don't invade and disrupt what God has joined together.

PRAYER. *God our Rock of refuge, protect and strengthen our marriage.*

 ACRED Scripture begins with the creation of man and woman in the image and likeness of God.

FEB.
1

—*Catechism of the Catholic Church,* 1602

Spitting image

REFLECTION. How often do we hear people approach a newborn baby and remark, "she looks just like her mother" or "he has his father's smile."

Man and woman are created in God's divine image and likeness. What attribute of your spouse is most divine to you? Seek the face of God in each other.

PRAYER. *Loving Father, allow Your image and likeness to be seen though our love for one another.*

WHAT does love look like? It has the hands to help others. It has the feet to hasten to the poor and needy. That is what love looks like.

—St. Augustine

FEB.
2

Hands, feet, and heart

REFLECTION. There have been some great movies from Hollywood romanticizing the love between a man and a woman.

In marriage the love story continues and while the romance we experienced at first may diminish, our hands, feet, eyes, and ears can all be utilized to love and serve.

PRAYER. *Jesus, let our love for one another be displayed in our service to each other.*

THE proof of love is in the works. Where love exists, it works great things. But when it ceases to act, it ceases to exist.

—Pope St. Gregory the Great

FEB.
3

Not by word alone

REFLECTION. Many who speak of love don't do very well at loving. Love has to be put into action.

Preparing meals, washing and ironing clothes, cutting the lawn, changing diapers can be external signs of love when we perform them without grumbling. Affirm in your spouse the "small things" they do with love.

PRAYER. *Loving Father, let our love never be just words but rather concrete actions.*

FOR where two or three are gathered together in my name, I am there in their midst. —Mt 18:20

Comfort and consolation

REFLECTION. In marriage two become one. There will be times as a couple that life seems overwhelming. The stress of paying bills, taking care of children and sometimes parents, and car trouble all seem to arrive at the same time.

Remember that you are not alone, Jesus is with you through it all. Trust in Him and in His timing.

PRAYER. *Lord, help us get through the daily grind of life by together turning to You.*

TWO are better than one.... For if they fall, one will lift up his fellow. —Eccl 4:9-10

FEB. 5

I will be there for you

REFLECTION. The Scripture speaks of the benefit of two rather than one which makes perfect sense. Sometimes our "falls" are not so evident. Disappointment at work, plans gone awry, and mild setbacks can be internal "falls."

Communicate every day in your marriage so you can pick each other up and offer support through it all.

PRAYER. *Holy Spirit, come to our aid as we come to the aid of each other.*

A SOUL enkindled with love is a gentle, meek, humble, and patient soul.
—St. John of the Cross

Four marks of love

REFLECTION. The Saints provide many examples of love both in their words and actions. In examining ourselves and our behavior towards our spouse we need to be open to the Holy Spirit who fills us with God's love.

How can we recognize a soul infused with love? Look for patience, humility, meekness and gentleness.

PRAYER. *Come Lord Jesus, arouse love within us and stir our love into a burning flame.*

S INCE God created them man and woman, their mutual love becomes an image of the absolute and unfailing love with which God loves man.
—*Catechism of the Catholic Church*, 1604

A reflection of God

REFLECTION. The Holy Trinity is a mystery. Yet the love between God the Father and God the Son introduces us to the Holy Spirit. It's the Holy Spirit who animates the love of God in human beings and this love is unfailing.

Rejoice that you are loved by God and each other and a model to others.

PRAYER. *Come Holy Spirit, awaken God's love for us and increase our love for one another.*

EVERY day there are ways for married couples to communicate love both with and without words. —George and Ida Daum

FEB.
8

Seek opportunities

REFLECTION. Married life, whether with children or without has its challenges. There never seems to be enough time, and we can be in danger of forgetting the love of our life.

Be creative in communicating love even if it's without a word. It's often the small things we do for one another that have the biggest impact.

PRAYER. *Jesus, our Redeemer, open our eyes to creative ways to communicate love.*

IT IS not so essential to think much as to love much. —St. Teresa of Jesus

FEB.
9

School of love

REFLECTION. Marriage is the great school of love where every day we have opportunities to excel in the subject of love. Hours of contemplation and study about love are not required as long as we put love into action.

An advanced degree in theology may look nice hanging on your office wall, but the real test comes in loving one another.

PRAYER. *Jesus, Mary, and Joseph, deepen our love for each other and for God.*

26

LL that we do is a means to an end, but love is an end in itself, because God is love.

—St. Teresa Benedicta of the Cross

Love is the goal

REFLECTION. In any athletic competition the end to be achieved is winning. We score points, runs, or goals to accomplish this.

St. Teresa (Edith Stein), a Carmelite Nun who was murdered at Auschwitz, reminds us that love is the goal in all things in the Christian life and she followed where love led.

PRAYER. *Lord God, help us to love and to keep that goal in the forefront of our lives.*

 EMEMBER Lot's wife. —Lk 17:32

Face forward

REFLECTION. Jesus referenced Lot's wife who "looked back" and turned into a pillar of salt. It's a solemn warning when we think of the person Jesus names. He does not ask us to remember Abraham, or Isaac, or Jacob, or Sarah, or Hannah, or Ruth.

In marriage as in life it's always good to look to the future and not dwell on the past.

PRAYER. *Jesus, our Good Shepherd, lead us forward together through all things.*

E HAS made everything beautiful in its time. —Eccl 3:11

FEB.

12

Through our Father's eyes

REFLECTION. Beauty, goodness and truth all give us a glimpse of the divine. Whatever God does He does perfectly. Sin causes our vision to be blurred and we fail to see the creator's hand in the creation.

Value the life you have, love your spouse for He has made everything beautiful in its time.

PRAYER. *Eternal Father, may our eyes be focused on You and attuned to Your voice.*

 PREAD love everywhere you go: first of all in your own house. —Blessed Mother Teresa

FEB.

13

Living room, bathroom, closet...

REFLECTION. Missionaries deserve our admiration for their willingness to spread God's word far from home. A good training ground for missionary service is our own home.

What a powerful witness married couples can provide for our society today. Let your love for one another overflow and watch the faith take root in society.

PRAYER. *Lord Jesus, may we both put our love into action in our home.*

OTHING attracts like love; love and you will win every heart.
—Blessed Pauline Von Mallinckrodt

Love is still number one

REFLECTION. Many commercials appeal to sex in order to promote their product. Wear this, drive that, drink this beverage and you will be attractive to the opposite sex. The underlying message is that sex is all we are made for.

It's love that fulfills our ultimate desires so continue to love one another in marriage with Jesus as our example of love.

PRAYER. *Loving Lord, help us see past the externals and to love with the heart of Jesus.*

 OUSE and wealth are inherited from fathers, but a prudent wife is from the Lord. —Prov 19:14

Head and heart in action

REFLECTION. Prudence is not a popular virtue nowadays yet it is essential to a successful marriage. The ability to reason is one thing but acting on it is another.

Thank God for the virtues your spouse has be it courage, patience, fortitude, and let them know you appreciate their gifts. Pray that in your marriage where one is weak the other is strong.

PRAYER. *Holy Spirit, be with us and increase our gifts to serve You and each other.*

ET brotherly love continue. Do not neglect to show hospitality to strangers, for thereby some have entertained angels unawares. **FEB. 16**
—Heb 13:1

Not just once or twice

REFLECTION. St. Paul expected the love between the believers to grow and points out that in being hospitable to strangers they have entertained angels. The "I do" on our wedding day is an ongoing "I do."

Let your love for one another continue for you just never know where that "I do" will lead you.

PRAYER. *Jesus, let our love be continual for each other and even for strangers in good times and in difficult times too.*

HIS grace of Christian marriage is a fruit of Christ's cross, the source of all Christian life. **FEB. 17**
—*Catechism of the Catholic Church, 1615*

A gift not earned

REFLECTION. In the Garden of Eden the relationship between God, man, and woman was severed. On the Cross Jesus repaired the harm done so we can go back to the beginning and live the way God intended.

Marriage between a man and woman is God's original plan and God gives us the grace to live it in joy.

PRAYER. *Dear God, pour out Your grace on our marriage and thank You for Your Son's life.*

EAL love is demanding.
—Pope St. John Paul II

Go for the real thing

REFLECTION. St. John Paul II speaks about the demanding nature of "real love." Real love sacrifices, real love is truthful, and real love dies to one's own needs so as to serve the other.

These demands however, allow us to live as God intended, and difficult as they can be, we find our true selves while loving.

PRAYER. *Our Blessed Mother, allow us to enjoy the fruits of real love through our marriage.*

 N THE threshold of his public life Jesus performs his first sign — at his mother's request — during a wedding feast.

—*Catechism of the Catholic Church*, 1613

A mother's view

REFLECTION. The Catholic Church honors Mary under numerous titles such as Our Lady of Mercy, Mother of Christ, Notre Dame and many more. It was Mary whose attention to detail initiated Jesus' first miracle at the Wedding at Cana.

Invite Mary to watch over your marriage and consecrate yourselves to her care for she desires the best for you.

PRAYER. *Mary, mother of Jesus, help us do whatever Jesus tells us to do in prayer.*

OVE alone counts.
—Blessed Pauline Von Mallinckrodt

The final score

REFLECTION. In sports you are judged by wins and losses and after the buzzer sounds that's all that matters. In marriage what matters is love and the quality of love we have for our spouse expressed through forgiveness, thoughtfulness, and faithfulness.

We may express it differently with words and without, but in the end it is the only thing that counts.

PRAYER. *Lord Jesus, may our love increase for You and each other every day.*

AVE everyone withdraw from me!
—Gen 45:1

Alone at last

REFLECTION. There will be occasions throughout your marriage that you need some time alone. This is not a rejection of your spouse but a simple fact that sometimes we need space to process the week's or day's events.

Be supportive of each other and give the space and time each other needs in order to come back renewed and refreshed.

PRAYER. *Lord God, refresh and renew us so we may be able to love as we ought.*

HERE the angel of the Lord appeared to him as fire flaming out of a bush.

FEB.
22

—Ex 3:2

The God of surprises

REFLECTION. God appeared to Moses while Moses was doing an ordinary task of the day, tending to his flock. How and why God appears to us at certain times of our lives may not be as extraordinary as Moses' encounter, but they can be just as real.

Be open to the Holy Spirit in your life and in your marriage in ordinary and extraordinary events.

PRAYER. *Come Holy Spirit, enliven our faith life together and surprise us with Your love.*

 ROM the communion sacrifice the individual shall offer as an oblation to the Lord the fat that covers the inner organs.

FEB.
23

—Lev 3:3

Give your best

REFLECTION. The Israelites believed that the inner organs were the best part of the animal, and when giving to God you want to give your very best.

Give your spouse the very best and offer your sacrifice of time, attention, and service to the one whom you love today and every day.

PRAYER. *God Almighty, when giving to our spouse may it always be our very best.*

33

THE one constant in our married lives is love and laundry.

—Mary and Brad Park

FEB.
24

Extraordinary and ordinary

REFLECTION. Young couples often wear "rose colored" glasses when imagining what married life is, and Hollywood movies certainly play up that end of love and romance.

Married people understand it's a long haul and that love is expressed in the bedroom but also in the laundry room and kitchen and through other mundane tasks. Do all this with love.

PRAYER. *Jesus, let me appreciate my spouse and show love in the ordinary tasks of life.*

THE Lord is with us. Do not fear them.

—Num 14:9

FEB.
25

Be not afraid

REFLECTION. The people of Israel were afraid and trusted in their own power instead of relying on God. Times of struggle and uncertainty will come to your marriage.

During those times make sure to take faith as your shield and God's Word as a sword. Stand together and be assured that there is no enemy too great for God.

PRAYER. *Loving Lord, when times get difficult send your Holy Spirit to strengthen and assure us of Your provision.*

HONOR your mother and your father.
—Deut 5:16

FEB.
26

Make them proud

REFLECTION. The Bible doesn't say to obey your parents in all things because our parents are human and they are fallible. It does however call us to honor them which means to live our lives in such a way that make them proud.

Whether they are living or deceased make honorable choices and live out your marriage in love.

PRAYER. *Lord Jesus, bless our marriage and thank You for the parents You gave us.*

WHO provides nourishment for the raven when it's young cry out to God, wandering about without food?
—Job 38:41

FEB.
27

God knows and cares

REFLECTION. It was believed that young ravens were not fed by their parents because they are white in appearance as newborns and unrecognizable as ravens.

If God in His provision takes care of these helpless, vulnerable birds how much more will our Loving Father provide for you who have made a commitment to love Him.

PRAYER. *Jesus, hear our prayers for our various needs and supply what we need.*

THE beginning of love is to let those we love be perfectly themselves, and not to twist them to fit our own image.

FEB. **28**

—Thomas Merton

Leave room for growth

REFLECTION. One of the biggest frustrations known to man is trying to force others to behave as we desire. Controlling behavior may work with children or pets but as adults we know we can't force people to change. The same is true in marriage.

Love your spouse in spite of their imperfections.

PRAYER. *Holy Spirit, transform our hearts and allow us to be the person God intended.*

WE ARE not some casual and meaningless product of evolution. Each of us is the result of a thought of God.

FEB. **29**

—Pope Benedict XVI

God knows your names

REFLECTION. Like any proud father, God has a true and intimate love for His children. In marriage you may experience the joy of having children, and you will most likely find yourselves staring at the wonder of this child entrusted to your care.

Be assured that God has an infinite love for both of you and delights in your presence.

PRAYER. *Loving Father, thank You for the gift of marriage and the joy of new life.*

GOD is our refuge and our strength, an ever present help in distress —Ps 46:2

Stress relief

REFLECTION. They say in the Catholic Church that when there is a wedding three get married for God is at the center of the couple's marriage. Sometimes God gets neglected and is gradually relegated to the sidelines.

Turn to Him often, cling to Him together for your faith in Him will see you through any distress.

PRAYER. *Our God, stay close to us as we stay close to You; be our strength in times of stress.*

TO LOVE and be loved by the one you love is everything.
—Bill and Pauline Beauregard

This one will last a lifetime

REFLECTION. At the heart of human beings is the desire to love and be loved.

Feelings will come and go but love as expressed through service, forgiveness, affection, and unconditional commitment to our spouse makes life worth living. Receiving love in return is the icing on the cake.

PRAYER. *Jesus, may our love for each other mirror our love for You.*

LOVE you, O Lord, my strength.

—Ps 18:2

MAR.
3

Eight simple letters

REFLECTION. We bring much of our family's influence and upbringing into our marriage. The way we communicate is often the biggest factor in how much couples grow together.

For some couples the daily affirmation of the words, "I love you," comes quite naturally while for others it's barely said. Say those words and say them often to your spouse.

PRAYER. *Heavenly Father, I love You and I love my spouse through thick and thin.*

WILL fear no evil, for you are at my side; your rod and your staff comfort me.

—Ps 23:4

MAR.
4

Rest easy

REFLECTION. Sheep will only lie down if they are well fed and protected. The Good Shepherd gives them this security for they know He is watching over them.

In the same way, assure your spouse of your constant care and protection. You will both rest easier knowing that God loves you and you love each other.

PRAYER. *Lord Jesus, thank You for giving us a shepherd's care night and day.*

ET him kiss me with the kisses of his mouth, for your love is better than wine.
—Song 1:2

MAR. 5

Kisses sweeter than wine

REFLECTION. *Eros* is but one of the four Greek words we translate as love. This word communicates beautifully the human desire for the opposite sex which is of course part of God's plan for a joy-filled marriage.

We long to give ourselves to our spouse as God longs to give Himself to us in Holy Communion.

PRAYER. *Loving Father, increase our desire for each other and may our love be fruitful.*

RAW me after you! Let us run!
—Song 1:4

MAR. 6

Overcome obstacles

REFLECTION. Early on in the Song of Songs we hear the bride exclaim, "Draw me after you." She is asking for help in overcoming any obstacle that might prevent oneness in their relationship.

The "running" together articulates beautifully her desire to partner with the King in the purpose and plan of their lives together. God desires the same with you.

PRAYER. *Loving Father, assist us in overcoming obstacles together and may we be united in heart and mind.*

ET US exult and rejoice in you; let us celebrate your love; it is beyond wine!

—Song 1:5

Intoxicating!

REFLECTION. Rejoicing and celebrating are part of God's plan for marriage. Love even goes beyond the intoxicating effects of wine. Love is safe for you can't give or receive too much.

Love never sours, produces no bad effects and it heals and provides joy. Rejoice in love and the one who loves you. Drink deep from the well of love.

PRAYER. *Gracious God, awaken our souls to love; pour out Your Spirit upon us.*

 ELL me, you whom my soul loves, where you shepherd, where you give rest at midday.

—Song 1:7

Love desires communion

REFLECTION. I doubt that many college students would use this line to ask a person out on a date: "Where do you shepherd?" In antiquity it was a way of communicating the desire to be in the other's presence.

Love still desires the presence, face to face with the other. Make time to be in God's presence and each other's.

PRAYER. *Holy Spirit, draw our hearts together as one and let us seek Your will for us.*

Y BELOVED is unto me as a cluster of henna in the vineyards of En-Gedi.
—Song 1:14

Protect and serve

REFLECTION. Henna was closely associated with human sexuality and love in the Old Testament. This would imply a metaphor for henna of a beloved who defends, shelters, and delights his lover.

Ensure that your marriage is well defended and protected through prayer and commitment and enjoy the security and freedom that love ensures.

PRAYER. *Lord, may our love be like "henna" which defends, shelters, and delights in love.*

 OW beautiful you are, my friend, how beautiful! Your eyes are doves!
—Song 1:15

I only have eyes for you

REFLECTION. Doves have binocular vision which means they can only focus on one thing at a time which is usually their mate. This has earned them the nickname of "love birds."

In the midst of busy schedules make the time to be love birds and focus on each other.

PRAYER. *Holy Spirit, descend upon us so we may focus on each other as You focus on us.*

41

OW beautiful you are, my lover, handsome indeed! —Song 1:16

Lavish with praise

REFLECTION. Our culture tends to praise almost everything from soft drinks to toilet tissue to award shows; everything receives praise.

When we reflect on what and who really matters in life our praise should be directed towards God and our spouse. Take the time each day to give praise where praise is due.

PRAYER. *Father of Mercy, we praise You and adore You for who You are.*

 AM a flower of Sharon, a lily of the valleys. —Song 2:1

Beautiful and humble

REFLECTION. Lilies are mentioned fifteen times in the Bible and they are the noblest of flowers. They grow tall yet hang their head down in humility. They are pure, beautiful, and one flower can contain over fifty bulbs.

Always view your spouse through the eyes of love and admire their beauty both inside and out.

PRAYER. *Loving God, remind us often of Your love for us and our love for one another.*

IKE a lily among thorns, so is my friend among women. —Song 2:2

One in a million

REFLECTION. It's pretty easy to discern a lily from a thorn for even a blind person can examine the two and come to a quick conclusion.

The beauty of a lily is seen both inside and out for every lily has seven seeds or grains which are not immediately seen. When the beauty of the outside fades the inside still retains its fruitfulness.

PRAYER. *Lord Jesus, may our outward appearance be exceeded by our growth in holiness.*

IKE an apple tree among the trees of the woods, so is my lover among men. —Song 2:3

Above and beyond

REFLECTION. The word we translate as lover in the Song of Songs appears twenty-four times in this biblical book and only twice elsewhere in the Old Testament. The intimate nature of love and the language of love drips from almost every verse.

Be generous with your praise and love towards one another and never fear to do a little extra.

PRAYER. *O Comforter, draw us into the heart of the Trinity so we may learn from You.*

E BROUGHT me to the banquet hall, and his glance at me signaled love.

—Song 2:4

The look of love

REFLECTION. One of the sweetest things to overhear are the words, "Did you see how they looked at each other?" When we are in love no words are needed and others can tell just by the way we look at one another.

God views us through the lens of love. Be attentive to your spouse and let your love shine through your eyes.

PRAYER. *Heavenly Father, forgive us the times we have failed to love You and each other.*

IS left hand is under my head, and his right arm embraces me. —Song 2:6

Life support

REFLECTION. Married life has various challenges and at times we may not even feel comfortable giving voice to the anxiety inside.

Assure one another that you are there for them, present and affirming throughout all that life may throw your way. Embrace each other and support one another with words and affection.

PRAYER. *Gracious God, thank You for the Holy Spirit who supports and strengthens us.*

Y LOVER speaks and says to me, **MAR.** "Arise, my friend, my beautiful one, and come!" —Song 2:10 **17**

Called by name

REFLECTION. Throughout the Song of Songs there is an appeal to the senses. Sight, smell, sound, and touch all play a part in communicating love.

In learning how our loved one responds we too can learn their love language and love them in concrete actions. A note, a text, or some other reminder goes a long way in deepening love.

PRAYER. *Jesus, communicate to us in a way that we can understand Your love for us.*

ET me see your face, let me hear your **MAR.** voice, for your voice is sweet and your face is lovely. —Song 2:14 **18**

Beautiful inside and out

REFLECTION. It's amazing how our voice inflection can impact the way our spouse hears our words. At times we may not be aware of it or even have the ability to control it because it's spontaneous.

Let our voices reflect the love we have for one another in gentleness and peace and help us to apologize for the times we are insensitive.

PRAYER. *Holy Spirit, release all anger and harshness from how we speak to one another.*

N MY bed at night I sought him whom my soul loves—I sought him but I did not find him. —Song 3:1

Seek and you will find

REFLECTION. How many of us as young adults longed to find our heart's desires, longed to love and be loved. In our spouse we have found that "other self." In the sacrament of marriage we asked God to bless our love and to assist us in growing in love.

Thank God for your husband or wife and rejoice that you have found your "other self."

PRAYER. *Beloved Father, draw us closer to You together and increase our love for each other.*

 IKE pomegranate halves, your cheeks behind your veil. —Song 4:3

Partially hidden

REFLECTION. The allure of the woman in the Songs of Songs is powerful. Her eyes, her voice, her hair and her face all draw the man to her. The man can only compare her to the most beautiful objects he has witnessed in nature and no doubt even those images fall short.

Be creative and fun in your affirmation of each other.

PRAYER. *Lord, Your love is beyond words but together we praise You as best we can.*

OU are beautiful in every way, my friend, there is no flaw in you.

—Song 4:7

Holy and wholesome

REFLECTION. Beauty plays an important role in love and attraction is what usually draws our attention to the other at first. In the Song of Songs there is beauty, there is desire, but the woman has also veiled herself—her humility is as captivating as her beauty.

Physical beauty is a gift from God but it cannot compare with the beauty of godly character.

PRAYER. *Jesus, may my beloved grow in holiness and may we present ourselves to You without a flaw.*

 OW much better is your love than wine, and the fragrance of your perfumes than any spice. —Song 4:10

Inebriating the senses

REFLECTION. Sight, smell, touch, and taste are all part of the romantic dance in courtship. Hours of preparation can go into how we present ourselves to the other to heighten our desirability.

Enjoy the gift of each other and rejoice that God desires that husband and wife are intimate.

PRAYER. *Our Blessed Mother, pray for us as we unite in heart, soul, and body.*

WAS sleeping but my heart was awake. **MAR.**
—Song 5:2
 23

Love ever attentive

REFLECTION. The name of God is never mentioned in the Song of Songs yet God is present in the love and lovemaking of the man and woman within the boundaries God has placed.

While procreation is one of the first commands of God, "be fruitful and multiply," God rejoices in the union of the husband and wife for unity's sake.

PRAYER. *Thank You Lord, in creating an ardent desire for Yourself and each other.*

 IS mouth is sweetness itself; he is **MAR.**
delightful in every way. —Song 5:16 **24**

He's a keeper

REFLECTION. Falling in love actually affects the intellectual areas of the brain through releasing euphoria-inducing chemicals which make us feel exhilarated about ourselves and the object of our affection.

As our love deepens and matures we find ourselves seeing and loving our beloved in new and different ways than we saw at first.

PRAYER. *Loving Father, may our marriage be a sign of true love in our delight of one another.*

OW beautiful you are, how fair, my love, daughter of delights. —Song 7:7

Love language

REFLECTION. Throughout the courtship in the Song of Songs we never hear a criticism or a discouraging word. We know that some marriages begin with praise and end in arguments for multiple reasons.

Could one reason be that we fail to speak the language of love and fail to build each other up? Have praise on your lips and correct gently in love.

PRAYER. *Lord, thank You for calling us Your children and for speaking tenderly to us through Jesus.*

ET me as a seal upon your heart . —Gen 45:4

Locked and loved

REFLECTION. A seal was used officially to give personal authority to a document and it functioned as an identification card.

In this case the seal is not forged in wax or clay but on the heart. Their mutually declared public love for one another is on display and both man and woman have a voice in declaring their love.

PRAYER. *Jesus, thank You for sealing us with Your Holy Spirit which stirs us to greater love.*

REMEMBER, your relationship is a sacrament, a visible sign of how Christ loved the Church. —Robert Standard

An outward sign

REFLECTION. Marriage is usually celebrated in the context of Mass after the couple has listened to the Word of God. With their mutual consent they become an image of Christ who gave His life for the Church.

Mass makes it obvious that the Eucharist is the source and summit of continuous nourishment for marriage.

PRAYER. *God Almighty, may our married lives be marked by love, service, and self-giving.*

IN LIFE we all make many mistakes, let us learn to recognize our errors and ask forgiveness. —Pope Francis

Contrition and confession

REFLECTION. It takes love to forgive but perhaps even greater humility to ask for forgiveness. It's the oil of a healthy relationship which soothes over the wounds and allows us to function as a couple and as a family.

We tend to replicate ourselves in our children; so model a forgiving heart at every offense.

PRAYER. *Merciful Father, remind us that there is no sin too great to be unforgiven.*

UT you, our God, are good and true, slow to anger, and governing all with mercy.

—Wis 15:1

MAR. 29

In the Divine image

REFLECTION. The closer we get to a mirror the more imperfections we see. Married life reveals the imperfections in both husband and wife.

As we try to become more like the One who created us, be patient with yourself and your spouse. You will have plenty of opportunities to be slow to anger and merciful each and every day.

PRAYER. *Jesus, the True Vine, may Your word take root in our lives and transform us.*

 ACOB was the father of Joseph, the husband of Mary.

—Mt 1:16

MAR. 30

You marry into a family

REFLECTION. One of the gifts and challenges of marriage is that you realize that you marry into a family. After you say "I do" your family usually doubles in size and includes mothers and fathers-in-law and a whole slew of relatives.

At times the Wisdom of Solomon is needed to navigate these relationships yet they all come as a gift.

PRAYER. *Lord, give me the strength and patience to love our whole family.*

51

HEN Joseph awoke, he did as the angel of the Lord had command-ed him. —Mt 1:24

The original strong and silent type

REFLECTION. St. Joseph is a remarkable man. Mentioned 18 times in the Scriptures he is righteous, obedient to God's word, protective of his wife and unborn child, and he does it all without saying a word.

Words can make a difference, but I'd rather have actions without words than words without actions any day.

PRAYER. *St. Joseph, may our actions be as yours, righteous, obedient, and full of love.*

 HEN they entered the house they saw the child with Mary his mother. —Mt 2:11

Open to new life

REFLECTION. The Wisemen were seeking Jesus and found Him in a home. It wasn't a syna-gogue or the Temple that the star shone over but a home. God makes His appearance in the small town of Bethlehem as an infant.

God desires to make His presence known in our homes today through our love for each member.

PRAYER. *Jesus, may our homes be a place where all who enter are loved and cared for.*

THERE is never a reason to lose hope; Jesus tells us He is with you until the end of the world. **APR. 2** —Pope Francis

Encouragement along the way

REFLECTION. We all are confronted with situations which we feel are hopeless, but our faith reveals that with God there is hope in even the most dire of circumstances.

Regaining trust, changing jobs, dealing with addictions can certainly push us to the edge, but the words of Jesus remain relevant and true, "I am with you always."

PRAYER. *Jesus, our Prince of Peace, may Your Spirit reassure us in times of hopelessness.*

MARRIED life is an adventure and only those who trust God for the future can really enjoy the ride. **APR. 3** —James and Becca White

And away we go!

REFLECTION. What we think we're getting into in marriage and what it turns out to be are usually two different things. Even living together before marriage can't replicate the commitment that sacramental marriage demands.

No need to worry because when God is central in your lives He is with you each step of the way.

PRAYER. *Lord God, be always present with us for we trust in You.*

53

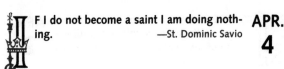 F I do not become a saint I am doing nothing.
—St. Dominic Savio

APR. 4

Holy innocence

REFLECTION. St. Dominic Savio was an ordinary boy who had an extraordinary love for God. Although he died at the young age of 15 he can be an example for all of us for we all are called to be Saints.

Married couples can work and pray together that they will assist their spouse in the way of holiness. The most difficult circumstances are occasions for virtue.

PRAYER. *Jesus, help us to see the trials and challenges of marriage as a way to holiness.*

 E CAN turn to God with our whole life because God is turning to us in Jesus. —Bishop Arthur Serratelli

APR. 5

Give and receive

REFLECTION. The sacrament of marriage is a mirror of the Holy Trinity. The love between the Father and Son is a model for us because they hold nothing back from each other and bear fruit in the Holy Spirit.

The love of the husband and wife can bear fruit in new life. It's foolish to hold back what we can't keep in order to gain what we cannot lose.

PRAYER. *Mary, pray for us as we desire to do whatever He tells us to do.*

MAN cannot live without love.
—Pope St. John Paul II

APR.
6

Come alive!

REFLECTION. At first glance the statement made by St. John Paul II may seem untrue for surely there are people who exist without love. The word "love" carries some weight in the biblical understanding for it's more than just having a pulse or blood pressure. It often means "come alive."

In marriage, love should ignite, come alive, and awaken life within us.

PRAYER. *Father, may our married life be attentive to those who are not loved.*

DISORDER in the society is the result of disorder in the family.
—St. Elizabeth Ann Seton

APR.
7

It begins in the home

REFLECTION. There is no perfect home but we should all strive for a healthy home. A home where grievances can be expressed, arguments can be talked about and mistakes forgiven.

Our marriage is the place where we set the tone for our family life, and the fruit of a healthy marriage is a healthy family and society.

PRAYER. *St. Joseph, assist us with keeping order, love, and Jesus at the heart of our marriage.*

FOR I was hungry and you gave me something to eat.

—Mt 25:35

8

Judgment day

REFLECTION. Jesus is clear that there will be a final judgment when we will all have to give an account of our lives. The belief we have in Jesus needs to be lived out each and every day.

Feeding and nourishing the poor can be something you do as a couple. Serving together creates a bond that lasts into eternity.

PRAYER. *Heavenly Father, provide opportunities for us to serve together and witness to love.*

———————

I WAS thirsty and you gave me something to drink.

—Mt 25:35

APR.
9

I thirst

REFLECTION. Beneath every crucifix in every convent, shelter, or home Mother Teresa founded, you will find the words, "I Thirst." Surely there are people who thirst for clean water but Mother Teresa said that Jesus thirsts for souls. His love is such that He thirsts for you and me.

Pray with and for your spouse daily as a gift to Jesus.

PRAYER. *Jesus, we come before You humbly and ask Your blessing upon us.*

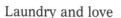 WAS naked and you clothed me.
—Mt. 25:36

APR.
10

Laundry and love

REFLECTION. God never wastes anything. Once we give it over to God it can be an avenue for love. That being said, most people see little love in laundry. It's not a bad problem to have when so many go through life with little or no clothing at all.

"Offer up" the inconvenience of doing the laundry for the sake of love.

PRAYER. *Lord God, help us be grateful for all we have and generous in donating what we don't use.*

_____

 ARRIAGE is about more than the flowers and the dress. —Pope Francis

APR.
11

Clothed in love

REFLECTION. There are different ways that marriages are celebrated around the country and around the world. While the preparations for the big day are important we should never lose sight of preparing ourselves for the life-long commitment.

It's not all about the dress, and long after the flowers fade you'll need faith to get you through.

PRAYER. *Our Lady of Good Counsel, may we model faithfulness in our marriage.*

MARRIAGE is a comprehensive act, an act that unites spouses at all levels of their humanity. —Pope Francis

Body, mind and spirit

REFLECTION. Our society often focuses on the sexual union between man and woman which is obviously very important. Pope Francis gently reminds us that there is more and that's a good thing.

We are giving our total selves to the other in marriage which includes the emotional, mental, and psychological as well as the psysical.

PRAYER. *Lord, let us freely give of ourselves to each other and hold nothing back.*

A COMPASS, a level, and a ruler remind us daily.—Joan and Paul Weller

APR. 13

Guideposts

REFLECTION. A compass shows direction, a level provides proper balance, and the ruler measures distance. How will you measure success in your marriage? Is there any part of your life that's out of balance? Are you going in the same direction?

There is never harm in asking the questions and in doing so you will have common goals that you can pursue together.

PRAYER. *Our Father, give us the common sense to communicate with each other so we're on the same page.*

EMBER how brief life is, and how weak you have made all mortals.

—Ps 89:48

APR.

14

Dust in the wind

REFLECTION. Ask any parent of a high school senior and the first words out of their mouth are, "I can't believe they're a senior! It went by in a flash."

Life does tend to go by quickly so it's worthwhile to take some time for yourself and your spouse every once in a while and to rejoice in the moment. Remember, even Jesus went off by Himself to pray.

PRAYER. *Heavenly Father, help us to make the most of each day and refresh us with Your Spirit.*

 AY your ears be attentive to my cry for mercy.

—Ps 130:2

APR.

15

It's too much for us

REFLECTION. Life is seldom like sailing on a crystal clear lake. There are periods of calm, but we know through experience that the storms will come and waves will appear.

When they come it seems that life may be overwhelming and there is no end in sight to the pain. It's during these times especially that we need to pray together and seek God's will.

PRAYER. *Lord, increase our faith especially when You seem most distant.*

WAIT with longing for the Lord, my soul waits for his word. —Ps 130:5

APR. 16

Waiting is the hardest part

REFLECTION. Waiting is a part of life. Researchers estimate that we spend about six months waiting in lines throughout our life. As children we wait for our parents, as married people we wait for each other.

Waiting for God is a part of faith which increases both our desire for Him and trust in Him. We can have confidence that God will act in His time.

PRAYER. *Mary, wait with us as we trust in the goodness of Your Son.*

 OW good it is, how pleasant where the people dwell as one. —Ps 133:1

APR. 17

One body in Christ

REFLECTION. When order and tranquility are part of our lives we can tend to take them for granted. When we walk into a situation where there is hostility, infighting, and discord we quickly realize how fortunate we are.

Let us strive for peace with one another and be mature in our response to discord whether it's our spouse, in laws, or relatives.

PRAYER. *Jesus our Good Shepherd, lead us in peace and help us dwell together in love.*

E'RE not always on the same page but always reading from the same book.

—Bernadette and Robert Petzinger

Love is patient, love is kind

REFLECTION. Disagreements and arguments are part of any relationship. The longer the relationship the more you will have. Those who navigate marriage successfully deal with them immediately and with honesty.

Don't be afraid to let the other know how you feel. Get it all out.

PRAYER. *Lord, help us to navigate our disagreements and to respond with love.*

 ARRIAGE is like dancing. You will fall out of step sometimes; getting back into rhythm quickly is key.

—Rebecca and John Schroppe

The greatest dance of my life

REFLECTION. Not every dance is the same and not every dancer is in tune with their partner. Marriage, like dance, takes time, patience, and practice to learn the rhythm and movement of the other.

The best dancers move in synchronicity, attuned to each other even in missteps, much like marriage.

PRAYER. *Holy Spirit, may we be attentive to Your movements and may we be in synch with You each step of our lives.*

IS call is demanding, because he invites you to let yourselves be "captured" by him completely.

APR.
20

—Pope St. John Paul II

Totally yours

REFLECTION. No one desires to be loved "part time." When we love we want to be loved 24/7. God calls us to love Him totally which seems demanding and at times impossible.

Marriage helps us to realize that it's not difficult to give ourselves totally to one we love and who loves us so much.

PRAYER. *Lord Jesus, we commit ourselves to put You first in our life and in our marriage.*

 F WE claim that we are sinless, we are only deceiving ourselves, and the truth is not in us.

APR.
21

—1 Jn 1:8

Reality check

REFLECTION. Through the lens of love our spouse is perfect which is not a bad thing. If we view ourselves as perfect, well, that's another story.

God's grace is available to help adjust our eyesight to see our imperfections. These imperfections and sins should not overwhelm us for God's mercy is available through the sacrament of reconciliation.

PRAYER. *Merciful Father, we acknowledge sin in our lives; help us to live in truth.*

HOEVER says he is in the light, yet hates his brother, is still in the darkness. —1 Jn 2:9

APR. 22

Out of step

REFLECTION. The Bible is very clear about forgiveness and leaving vengeance to the Lord but it can be so difficult to do. We want our "pound of flesh."

The problem is that hate can and will affect us in ways that may not be noticeable at first but will eventually seep into our marriage. Hate is never a God thing. Recognize it, confess it, and stay free.

PRAYER. *Lord God, grant me the grace to let go of hate and to grow in love.*

 WILL live the present moment to the fullest. —Cardinal Nguyen Van Thuan

APR. 23

The time is now

REFLECTION. Married couples know that much of their life is spent planning for future events. Vacations, education of children, and eventually retirement can have us constantly casting our eyes on the future.

Planning is prudent but there is wisdom in the advice of Cardinal Van Thuan, "live the present moment" and live it with gratitude

PRAYER. *Lord Jesus, remind us to enjoy the present moment at every stage of our lives.*

Y STRENGTH returns to me with my cup of coffee and the reading of the psalms. —Dorothy Day

Refresh and renew

REFLECTION. Married life can make demands on couples and affect them in different ways. At times we may feel that we're really in the groove, but after a while the groove becomes a rut.

Take care of yourself by adjusting your routine or maybe finding a good routine which will rejuvenate you. Whether alone or together it will make life easier.

PRAYER. *Jesus our hope, renew our strength with Your Word to face each day with joy.*

 EE what love the Father has bestowed on us that we may be called the children of God. —1 Jn 3:1

The apple of His eye

REFLECTION. One of the most reaffirming images of God is that of Father. It's an image used by the authors of the Old Testament in describing how God functions and is used by Jesus Himself.

The love of God the Father is the model for all fathers to aspire to. In meditating on the Scriptures we can grow more closely into the father God calls men to be.

PRAYER. *Holy Spirit, guide us in the vocation of fatherhood that we may imitate God.*

EEK first the kingdom of God and his righteousness, and all these things will be given to you besides. —Mt 6:33

APR. 26

One thing is needed

REFLECTION. Socrates said that the unexamined life is not worth living, but it's easier to live that way. If we examine our lives we might realize we need to change. The examined life takes time. It takes a receptive heart.

Jesus calls us to put Him first in our lives and in our marriage. When is the last time you examined your faith in Christ together?

PRAYER. *Jesus, we commit to putting You first in all areas of our lives and to trust in Your provision.*

 ISTEN to counsel and receive instruction, that you may eventually become wise. —Prov 19:20

APR. 27

Acquired over time

REFLECTION. In so many aspects of life we seek out others for advice and instruction. Whether it be in sports or school or on-the-job training we desire the wisdom of others to advance and be the best we can be.

Marriage is no different if we want to excel. Listen and learn from those who have successfully navigated marriage in good times and in bad.

PRAYER. *Blessed Mary, help us to have a holy family where we grow in holiness and love.*

AVE the child and you save all.
—Rev. Thomas A. Judge

APR.
28

Protect, guide, and love

REFLECTION. How do you spell love to a child? TIME. We give our time to people and things that we deem important. We are lucky to "grab a few minutes" with the boss or to "invest our time" in studying.

Give the greatest gift parents can give, the gift of time.

PRAYER. *Merciful Father, we pray for parents who neglect to spend time with their children.*

T'S easier to build strong children than to fix broken men.
—Frederick Douglas

APR.
29

Invest your time

REFLECTION. Frederick Douglas stated beautifully a truth that was as accurate in the 1800s as it is today. So many men and women who struggle with drugs, relationship problems, addictions, and who are incarcerated can trace the root of their issues to their father or lack thereof.

We can't begin to imagine the value and benefit of loving parents.

PRAYER. *God our Father, equip us to provide love, discipline, and guidance to our children.*

MILD answer turns back wrath, but a harsh word stirs up anger. —Prov 15:1

Nothing really changes

REFLECTION. Anger is quite natural and we see Jesus Himself in the Temple angry at the money changers for making a mockery of the Temple. How we express anger with poverty, injustice, and hunger in the world may take various forms.

When it comes to relationships and especially in marriage the advice from Proverbs is without a doubt the way to go.

PRAYER. *Jesus, stir Your Holy Spirit within us so we are loving in our speech.*

 LESSED is the man who does not walk in the counsel of the wicked, nor stand in the way of sinners. —Ps 1:1

Stand by me

REFLECTION. The sins of our culture can find their way into the Church and into our lives if we don't keep a vigilant watch. Not everything in our culture is bad but many of the values we see displayed through the television, internet, and in certain people are not of God.

Walk together and stand together in the way of the Lord and avoid the drama.

PRAYER. *Loving Father, let us never stray from Your side nor walk away from Your way.*

ATHER, his delight is in the law of the Lord, and on that law he meditates day and night. —Ps 1:2

MAY 2

Twenty-four seven

REFLECTION. Pleasure, happiness, and joy are all words associated with "delight." The author of the Psalms speaks about a blessed person who delights in God's law and ponders them day and night.

God communicates to us through His Word, His "love letter" to us. Read His love letter together and allow His Word to take root in your heart.

PRAYER. *Merciful God, thank You for the gift of Your Word; speak to us together.*

E IS like a tree planted near streams of water, which bears fruit in its season. —Ps 1:3

MAY 3

God works through you

REFLECTION. Various conditions need to be met for a plant or tree to bear fruit. The most essential element perhaps is water. The exterior of the plant or tree will be healthy and bear fruit only if the roots, which are usually hidden, reach deep down in fertile, moist soil.

Married couples can thrive when their lives are rooted in the heart of God the Father.

PRAYER. *God, our Father, let us draw close to You no matter what season we are in.*

THE definitive love that can truly become this "second wine" is more wonderful still; it is better than the first wine. And this is what we must seek.

—Pope Benedict XVI

Where love goes, wine flows

REFLECTION. The Pope described falling in love as the start of a couple's journey, not its highest point. Something "more wonderful still" awaits the couple.

At the wedding feast of Cana the first wine is very fine and this is falling in love, but it does not last until the end. A second wine has to come later, it has to ferment and grow, to mature.

PRAYER. *Thank You Lord, guide us as we mature in our love through all its stages.*

WHEN I call upon you, answer me, O God. — Ps 4:2

Waiting is the hardest part

REFLECTION. In every marriage there are ups and downs. Forces both external and internal can cause stress on individuals and therefore marriages. It's vitally important to take every situation that causes stress and anxiety to God in prayer.

With faith we leave the answer to God's timing and trust in His provision for us in all things great and small.

PRAYER. *Jesus, we trust in You and wait patiently and faithfully for Your answer.*

EAR my cry for help, my King and my God; for to you I pray. —Ps 5:3

In God we trust

REFLECTION. The author of the Psalms, King David, was a man after God's own heart and was anointed King of Israel. Time and time again throughout the Psalms we read of his "cry" to the Lord.

King David reminds us that those who believe are not immune from fear or disaster. We are also reminded to cry out to the Lord when trouble approaches.

PRAYER. *Lord Jesus, we cast our cares on You as You care for us through thick and thin.*

 AMILIES are built up by the ability to forgive and seek forgiveness.
—Pope Benedict XVI

Build a dynasty that continues

REFLECTION. Jesus often links receiving forgiveness with the ability to forgive others. When we recognize how often we misspeak, fail to act, and need forgiveness from others and God, it should cause us to be more sensitive and forgiving to others.

In marriage, the "other" is your spouse. Forgive and seek forgiveness often, from the heart.

PRAYER. *Forgiving Lord, You never tire of forgiving us as we forgive each other.*

THERE is much suffering because there is so very little love in homes and in family life. —St. Mother Teresa

Home is where the hurt is

REFLECTION. What difference does participating in Mass and receiving the Eucharist make? It makes all the difference in the world when we realize that how we love and how we live should be a reflection of God's love for us.

We need to be reminded weekly at Mass and then imitate the one whom we receive in the Eucharist. Let His love overflow in your family.

PRAYER. *Lord Jesus, as You give Yourself to us may we give of ourselves to our family.*

I WILL recount all your wondrous deeds. —Ps.9:2

No one outdoes God in generosity

REFLECTION. Human nature tends to focus on what went wrong. If you give a talk where ninety-nine people praise you and only one criticizes you, you will usually focus on the one who made the negative comment. We tend to act that way with God as well.

God is open to our questioning and complaints, but take time each day as a couple to thank Him.

PRAYER. *Lord, may we always be mindful of the blessings in our lives and return to give thanks to You.*

NO CHRISTIAN, whether or not he is called to the married state, has a right to underestimate the value of marriage. —St. Josemaria Escriva

MAY 10

The work of God

REFLECTION. **The Church only recognizes a few Saints who were married. While not diminishing the heroic and virtuous lives of priests, religious sisters and brothers who witnessed to the faith in extraordinary ways, it speaks of a mindset that only the ordained are called to be Saints.**

In fact, we are all called to be Saints in the state of life God has called us.

PRAYER. *Lord God, help us to sanctify each other and encourage each other to be Saints.*

FOR John baptized you with water, but within a few days you will be baptized with the Holy Spirit. —Acts 1:5

MAY 11

Stir into flame the gift of God

REFLECTION. **The Holy Spirit was promised by Jesus to His disciples and He is the greatest gift Jesus could have given to His church. The Spirit is the "breath of God" or *Ruah* in Hebrew. God breathed life into Adam.**

In restoring all things to their rightful place, God pours out His Spirit to those who believe in order to enjoy life as God intended.

PRAYER. *Lord, what was disrupted by sin restore by Your Holy Spirit stirring in each of us.*

72

OD raised this Jesus to life. Of that we are all witnesses. —Acts 2:32

MAY 12

Take the witness stand

REFLECTION. **Pope St. Paul VI said, "People are more impressed by witnesses than they are by teachers." Sacramental marriage provides a witness to God's love and fidelity which gets lived out each day in the lives of the married couple.**

Give witness to who Jesus is in your life in word and deed for so many miss out on the joy of what authentic love is.

PRAYER. *Lord God, may our love and fidelity be a public witness to Your plan for marriage.*

HEY devoted themselves to the teaching of the apostles and to the communal fellowship, to the breaking of bread and to prayers. —Acts 2:42

MAY 13

These four things

REFLECTION. **These four actions can be witnessed in any Catholic Church around the world. Marriages flourish when these are put into practice in the home, and family life thrives when these are lived out.**

Our Sunday ritual will come to full expression when the faith is lived out in the home. In such homes married couples support each other and parents witness to the children.

PRAYER. *Heavenly Father, may we be as devoted to following Your will as the early Christians.*

LET God be God and your spouse be human. —Mary and Sam Wilson

Without shining armor

REFLECTION. It can be difficult to accept the fact that your spouse is not perfect. This is not to say that we shouldn't try our best for the one we love but unrealistic expectations only lead to frustration that can fracture a relationship.

Value your spouse for who they are and love them where they are at. Only God is perfect.

PRAYER. *Lord Jesus, forgive me for the times I have been too demanding on my spouse and too easy with myself.*

ONLY through sexual difference can a man and woman "speak" the language of married love in and through their bodies: the complete and total gift of self. —USCCB

Creative differences

REFLECTION. The word we use for "rib" in the book of Genesis is used in many other places in Scripture and is often translated as "side." Imagine the joy Adam experienced when he first fixed his gaze upon Eve. Finally, a person similar to himself with some creative differences.

How true it is when spouses speak of "my better half" for together they complete each other.

PRAYER. *God Almighty, may we always be appreciative of the gift that we are to each other.*

APPRECIATE each new day together. Take nothing for granted. Say I love you every time you leave the house.
—Becky and David Stambaugh

MAY
16

Good news bears all

REFLECTION. "Another day, another dollar." "Same old same old." Every once in a while we are jarred out of our complacent lifestyle when disaster strikes and our world gets turned upside down.

It's good to re-evaluate just who and what are important to us so we never take each other or life for granted. After reading this turn to your spouse and say, "I love you."

PRAYER. *Loving Lord, we appreciate each other and together we thank You for everything.*

 THEN Peter grasped him by the right hand and helped him to get up.
—Acts 3:7

MAY
17

I will be there for you

REFLECTION. The actions of St. Peter in the Acts of the Apostles can be lived out every day in a married couple's life. We all experience setbacks and failures and the "world" can knock us down now and again.

Isn't it great that we can offer a helping hand to each other! Maybe it's a hand or a glass of wine or a show of affection that will pick our spouse up.

PRAYER. *Lord Jesus, You reached out to raise St. Peter out of the sea, help us to remember to reach out to each other.*

THE entire community of believers were united in heart and soul. —Acts 4:32

MAY 18

Shake it off

REFLECTION. The early Christian community experienced hardship and persecution for the first three hundred years of its existence. How did they survive? The New Testament speaks of unity of heart and soul.

Married couples will inevitably face hardships and difficulties. We weather them as did the early Church—unity with each other in Christ.

PRAYER. *Lord Jesus Christ, keep us united through mutual prayer and sacrifice for each other.*

WHEN one lives attached to money, pride or power, it is impossible to be truly happy. —Pope Francis

MAY 19

Detach to attach

REFLECTION. There is pressure in our society to go after the money, the big bucks, and all that can come with it. Many college students choose careers based on financial compensation alone which leads down a path which is difficult to leave.

When we have Christ at the center of our lives and choose to live our life together for Him, we will experience true joy.

PRAYER. *Our Father, help us detach from this world in order to attach to You and each other.*

THE apostles gave the name Barnabas, meaning "son of encouragement."

—Acts 4:36

MAY 20

Name changer

REFLECTION. Barnabas is mentioned twenty-five times in the New Testament and was a close companion to St. Paul. The community thought so highly of this man's character that they changed his name.

How valuable is it to have an encouraging person on the team, in the workplace, or at home. Appreciate the encouraging people in your life or better yet, be one.

PRAYER. *Holy Spirit, help us encourage each other and to be each other's biggest fan.*

PETER and the other apostles replied, "We must obey God rather than men."

—Acts 5:29

MAY 21

Whom will we serve?

REFLECTION. In the Bible, obedience and love go hand in hand. St. Thomas Aquinas tells us that it's more important to love God than to know Him, since he who is joined to God by love, is one spirit with Him.

Our knowledge of God and what He requires of us will set us apart from others because that's what love requires. May our marriage always be united to Christ through love.

PRAYER. *Loving God, give us strength to follow You and be obedient to Your Word.*

77

ELL-ORDERED self-love is right and natural. —St. Thomas Aquinas

MAY 22

Love God's creation

REFLECTION. Humility is not thinking less of yourself but thinking of yourself less. Yet how many times do people allow themselves to be treated less than they deserve? Even Christians can misinterpret humility and allow themselves to be treated like doormats.

Remind your spouse of the dignity you both have and rest assured that you are called to love yourself.

PRAYER. *Jesus, overwhelm us with Your love for us and let that love overflow into our relationship.*

 AVE I loved you enough today? —Fr. Richard Carton

MAY 23

Today and every day

REFLECTION. Parish priests are on the front line in meeting with couples who wish to get married in the Church. The question posed is a rich question because it begs for an honest answer. It is a generous question because it calls us to stretch a little further.

Go ahead, ask your spouse: *Have I loved you enough today?* After all, love endures forever.

PRAYER. *Father, each day may we be able to answer "yes" to our spouse.*

MY GOD, I love you!
—St. Thérèse of Lisieux

Last words of a Saint

REFLECTION. Sometimes we have the chance to say our last words to people. Maybe it's a few words in a high school yearbook or a farewell speech at a retirement party. And then there are those times that we wished we had known it would be the last time.

Tomorrow is never promised. Let your spouse know you love them each and every day.

PRAYER. *Jesus, we love you! May Your love compel us to share that love.*

THE examination of conscience we make before going to confession makes us face the truth about ourselves. —Bishop Arthur Serratelli

Can we handle the truth?

REFLECTION. The sacrament of reconciliation is vital for a healthy marriage and a balanced life. Most people don't take advantage of it because it is perhaps too difficult for them to live an examined life.

When we humbly examine ourselves and confess our sins we hear His word of forgiveness. We begin anew and through this assurance of being loved and forgiven we become better spouses.

PRAYER. *Lord Jesus, help us admit our sins in this sacrament so we may be free to love.*

MARRIAGE is like a roller coaster with lots of twists, turns, and ups and downs. What a blessing to have the one that you love beside you on the ride. —John and Suzanne Sarisky

MAY 26

Roller coaster of love

REFLECTION. We can go through almost anything in life as long as we know we are not alone. Even if someone is not physically present we can be assured that they are with us in spirit.

The opposite is true for we can feel alone even in marriage. During the twists and turns of married life over-communicate your love for your spouse.

PRAYER. *Loving Lord, be a part of every twist and turn of our marriage.*

EVEN if a unity of faith is not possible, a unity of love is. —Hans Urs von Balthasar

MAY 27

A harmony in my heart

REFLECTION. Jesus said that people will know that you are His disciples by our love for one another. Too often people seek what divides them rather than those things which bring them together.

Theologians argue among themselves as do married couples about what they believe. When there are disagreements, don't let love be diminished.

PRAYER. *Heavenly Father, may we always be united in love, if not faith.*

OVE is therefore the fundamental and innate vocation of every human being.

—Pope St. John Paul II

MAY 28

Heart speaks to heart

REFLECTION. Married life affords us opportunities to answer love's call in beautiful and sacrificial ways. Love is the longing of our inmost being; it's what we are made for.

When we learn what authentic love is from Jesus and enter into the mystery of that love we can begin to die to ourselves, our ego, and allow love to take root and blossom.

PRAYER. *Loving Father, we surrender our whole selves to Your will.*

 STILL miss him every day but I have faith that death does not have the final word.

—Sarah Connor

MAY 29

Death is not the final answer

REFLECTION. The refrain of a popular country song states, "He stopped loving her today." The sentiments are beautiful as it recalls a man who never got over a broken heart and stopped loving her only when he died.

As Christians we take another view of death for Jesus conquered death and promises us eternal life. We value each day on earth but know there is more.

PRAYER. *God Almighty, thank You for each day that we have together both now and in eternity.*

FEAR is the enemy of love. —St. Augustine **MAY**
30

Trapped in fear

REFLECTION. Perfect love casts out fear for when we entrust ourselves to the care of another we do so in faith. It's God to whom we are asked to trust our present and future lives.

When we do this we are then free to love and embark on the great mystery of married love where we entrust ourselves to another knowing God has our future in His hands.

PRAYER. *Mary, our Blessed Mother, be a mother to us as we entrust ourselves to your Son.*

LOVE seeks one thing only: the good of the one loved. It leaves all the other secondary effects to take care of themselves. **MAY**
—Thomas Merton **31**

Trust in love, seek and restore

REFLECTION. Our spouse should be the recipient of the results of our love for God. The results or the "fruits" that we enjoy for trusting God are love, joy, peace, patience, kindness, gentleness, and self-control.

When we abandon ourselves to divine love we may not know where we are going but we know who we are going with.

PRAYER. *Lord, let us seek You in all things trusting in Your love and provision for us.*

HEN the angel said to her, "Do not be afraid, Mary, for you have found favor with God. —Lk 1:30

Approval granted

REFLECTION. New beginnings in life are cause for excitement as well as some anxiety. Whatever phase of married life we are in there are always new beginnings. A new home, a new pregnancy, a new job, a new school, and the list goes on.

The same God who assures Mary to "be not afraid" is with you as well in your marriage and desires that your joy may be complete.

PRAYER. *Come Holy Spirit, walk beside us and guide us each step of our lives.*

EHOLD, you will conceive in your womb and bear a son, and you will name him Jesus. —Lk 1:31

The blessing of pregnancy

REFLECTION. Married couples seeking to become pregnant quickly realize that pregnancy is not always a given. Medical issues, miscarriages, and other factors can hit married couples hard, wife and husband alike.

We recognize that God is involved in the process and each life, whether that life comes to full term or not, is a gift to be cherished.

PRAYER. *Mary, pray for us as we cooperate in bringing children into this world.*

ET it be done to me according to your word. —Lk 1:38

Mary's "fiat" in faith

REFLECTION. Imagine the pure joy Mary experienced in having Jesus at her breast nursing, holding Him asleep in her arms, and feeding Him His first bites of table food. Joseph was there also holding His little hand and doing things that dads do.

Saying "yes" to God requires trust by parents in both God and in one another. It's the road less traveled.

PRAYER. *Heavenly Father, may our marriage and life always be a "yes" to Your Word.*

Y SOUL proclaims the greatness of the Lord and my spirit rejoices in God my Savior. —Lk 1:46-47

JUNE 4

Mary's eyes were fixed on God

REFLECTION. Catholics have not done a great job of articulating the faith. It seems religion or faith is considered a private matter. This is utter nonsense.

Our example as married Catholics is Mary who was not afraid to boldly proclaim what God, the Lord, the Mighty One, the Savior has done for her. Be a couple for Christ and never be shy about what God has done for you.

PRAYER. *Holy Spirit, give us courage and opportunities to share our faith in confidence and joy.*

OSEPH therefore went from the town of Nazareth in Galilee to Judea, to the city of David called Bethlehem. —Lk 2:4

Protective love of wife and child

REFLECTION. St. Joseph was a real "man's man" and an excellent example for men today. Despite difficult circumstances his love for his wife and unborn child was on display even though he is not recorded as saying a word.

Who needs words when your actions can speak for you? How are you putting your love in action for your spouse and children?

PRAYER. *St. Joseph, pray for us as we show protective, unconditional love for each other.*

OR the love of Christ urges us forward. —2 Cor 5:14

No going back

REFLECTION. One of the most famous lines from the 1970s movie "The Exorcist" was, "The power of Christ compels you." To be compelled is to be so strongly moved or convicted about something that you have no other choice but to speak or act.

Married life in Christ urges us to move forward, move forward together, and move forward in love.

PRAYER. *Merciful Father, help us to move forward in all circumstances for with You there is hope.*

MARRIAGE imagery is central in describing God's covenant with Israel and, later, the Church.
—2015 World Meeting of Families

JUNE 7

I love you like…

REFLECTION. Often words aren't enough to describe an experience such as a sunset, a waterfall, or some other encounter that takes our breath away. Words, we know, can fall short.

God, in communicating to us His children, uses the imagery of marriage multiple times in Scripture to convey His love, His desire, and His faithfulness to us.

PRAYER. *Lord God, You speak of marriage to reveal Your love. May love be revealed in our marriage.*

THE marriage between God and His people can be rocky!
—2015 World Meeting of Families

JUNE 8

Unpredictable but never unfaithful

REFLECTION. Throughout the Old Testament, we read of a tumultuous relationship between God and His people that would fit right in with any modern television reality show.

Relationships have their ups and downs. God is our example of the perfect spouse for He is faithful and loving through it all.

PRAYER. *Lord Jesus, may we always be there for each other as You are always there for us.*

OUR single endeavor should be to give ourselves to the work and to be faithful to him. —St. Isaac Jogues

Accomplishment or activity

REFLECTION. Married life will have many challenges along the way. When children are part of the picture schedules multiply exponentially. Before we realize it, husband and wife are heading in a dozen different directions.

St. Isaac Jogues was focused on God and his mission. What is separating you from God and spouse?

PRAYER. *God, may we have the wisdom to commit our time to the most essential people each day.*

LOVE demands effort and a personal commitment to the will of God. —Pope St. John Paul II

Absolute beginners

REFLECTION. There are over 14,000 songs with the word "love" in the title. Rarely, if ever, do artists croon about the demands of love or commitment to the will of God. They should!

In loving according to God's will and disciplining ourselves to conform to love's demands, we begin to live! In dying to ourselves we allow space for God, space for love.

PRAYER. *Lord, reveal Your will to us so we may love perfectly and according to Your will.*

HAVE endured toil and hardships and sleepless nights. —2 Cor 11:27

Ah, the joys of parenthood

REFLECTION. St. Paul endured many hardships in proclaiming the Good News of Jesus and some of them are familiar to parents today. Few things are as joyful, beautiful, delightful, *and* disruptive as a child.

Sleep? Forget about it. Keeping to your schedule? Not a chance. However, when love abounds and communication is open you can savor it together.

PRAYER. *Lord, when we are exhausted and sleep evades us, renew us in strength and humor.*

 ARRIAGE to us is about honesty. If we have a problem...my wife lets me know. —Joanie and Bill Cioffi

Dynamite

REFLECTION. It can take the Wisdom of Solomon to know when to speak and when to keep silent in any relationship, let alone marriage.

When we keep issues buried inside and avoid controversy at all cost we can tell ourselves it's out of love that I bury these feelings which may end up doing more harm than good. Make honesty a hallmark of your marriage.

PRAYER. *Lord God, may we never fear to speak the truth in love and honesty.*

Y GRACE is sufficient for you, for power is made perfect in weakness.
—2 Cor 12:9

JUNE 13

Fill up what is lacking

REFLECTION. St. Paul was perhaps the greatest evangelist to ever live. Two-thirds of the New Testament contain his writings. This great Saint was aware of the fact that he couldn't do it all and what was lacking in his life was filled by the Spirit of God.

Married couples help do that for each other, they fill what is lacking in each other making the other whole.

PRAYER. *Lord, may we be filled with the Holy Spirit and experience Your Power in our lives.*

EAR of the Lord is the beginning of knowledge, fools despise wisdom and knowledge.
—Prov 1:7

JUNE 14

A healthy respect for God

REFLECTION. Lawyers often remark that a man who is his own lawyer has a fool for a client. The point being that we need the humility to accept counsel from others.

A name for the Holy Spirit in Greek is *paráklētos* which is a legal term applied to someone who stands beside you to defend you. Call the Holy Spirit to your side; He will give you counsel.

PRAYER. *Come Holy Spirit, teach us wisdom and stand beside us as we stand beside each other.*

UT whoever obeys me dwells in security, in peace, without fear of harm.
—Prov 1:33

Stay, stay, stay

REFLECTION. In freedom, God allows us to do whatever we desire to do, good or bad, for you can't force someone to love you. God knows what is best for us because He created us.

Emotionally, psychologically, mentally…every aspect of our humanity God created. When we obey God we find a certain freedom, a peace that surpasses all understanding.

PRAYER. *Loving Father, in reading and hearing Your word may we obey it and find peace.*

 N ALL your ways be mindful of him and he will make straight your paths. —Prov 3:6

Always on my mind

REFLECTION. There is a temptation to relegate to God only certain areas of our lives which we feel He should be involved in. Many "cultural" Catholics give God a few hours each year during Christmas and Easter and God is not in their thoughts until next year or when a crisis arises.

God has the very best for all aspects of life; always be mindful of Him.

PRAYER. *Lord, forgive us for those times when You were an afterthought; keep us focused.*

ER ways are pleasant ways, and all her paths are peace. —Prov 3:17 **JUNE 17**

She has a way about her

REFLECTION. Wisdom is personified as a woman in the book of Proverbs and is spoken about with terms of affection and joy.

When we have God in the center of our lives and when God's wisdom is sought after as a couple, life reveals the result or the "fruit" of the Christian marriage which is peace. Peace with God and one another.

PRAYER. *Blessed Mother, Our Lady of Peace, increase our love for Jesus in our lives.*

 HY did I not listen to the voice of my teachers, incline my ear to my instructors. —Prov 5:13 **JUNE 18**

Death or glory

REFLECTION. Some of our most valuable teachers and instructors have never stepped a foot inside a classroom to teach.

If we look around us we are bombarded with magazine headlines, social media "feeds," and examples of others who offer us instruction of what to do and not do. Learn from the successes as well as the missteps of others.

PRAYER. *Lord, may we learn from those around us and avoid missteps in our marriage.*

IND them on your fingers, write them on the tablet of your heart. —Prov 7:3

With this ring…

REFLECTION. The wedding ring is the outward sign of married life to the world. It's located right where others can see it plainly. The conjugal love of the couple unites them in body and heart, the two are one flesh.

So intimately does God desire to love us that He sent His Spirit to "seal" us in His love. Never be ashamed to speak of His love for you or your love for one another.

PRAYER. *Lord Jesus Christ, You gave Your life for us, may we lay down our lives for each other.*

HE Bible is essential and we share the Word of God every week. We strengthen and transform our community through prayer. —Fr. Joseph Healey, MM

The original small Christian community

REFLECTION. Fr. Healey has spent over fifty years in Africa and abroad forming and supporting small Christian communities.

The family is the original small Christian community where the faith is lived, encouraged, supported, and nourished by God's Word and prayer. In what ways are faith supported and lived out in your marriage, in your family?

PRAYER. *Jesus, may our family pray together and be strengthened by Your Word.*

THE Holy Spirit will show us the way through whatever human muddle we may be in at the moment.

—Fr. Joseph Healey, MM

We are not alone

REFLECTION. Lawyers, judges, and magistrates have access to the chambers of the court where dialogue can take place, compromises made, and justice dispensed.

Whatever "muddles" our marriage we have an Advocate who speaks for us in the chambers of the Sacred Heart of Jesus. We indeed have a friend in high places who speaks for us.

PRAYER. *Assist us Holy Spirit during those times when life gets difficult and problematic.*

HATRED stirs up disputes, but love covers all offenses.

—Prov 10:12

Operator's Manual

REFLECTION. Quite often in marriage and in other relationships we come to a crossroads. It may not be a life or death situation but we inevitably make decisions which either help or hinder the growth of our relationship.

Sometimes we choose poorly and hurt the one we love. We then face a new choice. Do we choose to love after we harmed someone or when we ourselves were hurt?

PRAYER. *Lord God, may our encounter with You overflow into all aspects of our marriage.*

FOR lack of guidance a people falls, security lies in many counselors. —Prov 11:14

JUNE 23

All lost in the supermarket

REFLECTION. The self-made person is greatly admired in America. While this can be a good thing we can forget our dependence on God and on others.

In marriage we have to make many choices and when we remember that we have the wisdom and counsel of others available to us we should not feel like a lost child in the supermarket. Use the counsel of others to move forward.

PRAYER. *Jesus, remind us that we belong to a community so we never have to face trials alone.*

"**M**AY I?" "Thank you." "Forgive me." —Pope Francis

JUNE 24

Recipe for joy

REFLECTION. Pope Francis said that these three statements are fundamental for a happy family life. When these words are missing the Pope commented, "It's no joke."

How many opportunities will we have to use these words today? How many times do we say these same words to God? Use these words frequently both with God and your spouse.

PRAYER. *Lord, thank you. Forgive me. May we use these words every day.*

SOMETIMES a way seems right, but the end of it leads to death. —Prov 14:12

JUNE 25

Decisions, decisions, decisions

REFLECTION. The book of Proverbs mentions "counsel" many times and there is certainly wisdom in seeking godly advice. We know however that even the best laid plans fail. Unforeseen circumstances, forces beyond our control can devastate us.

We have an advantage over our Old Testament ancestors. The assurance of hope in Jesus Christ.

PRAYER. *Lord, guide our steps as we seek to do Your will. May our plans be according to Your will.*　　　——————

THE ill-tempered stir up strife, but the patient settle disputes. —Prov 15:18

JUNE 26

Just a little patience

REFLECTION. Throughout the book of Proverbs we read about comparisons between the wise and the foolish, the wealthy and the poor, the industrious worker and the slacker, and so on.

It may be easy to see imperfections in others but difficult to see them in ourselves which is why humility is so important. Reflect on your own flaws and pray for the grace to change.

PRAYER. *Lord, be patient with us both as we allow You to transform us inwardly.*

SEE everything, overlook much, and correct a little.
—Pope St. John XXIII

Saintly advice

REFLECTION. A good friend of mine is the voice of a NFL football team. He does an excellent job describing the scene, the players, the formation, and the play in great detail for the radio audience. When the game is over he stops commentating.

The Pope's advice is good for marriages as well, only I might add, affirm often and encourage always.

PRAYER. *Jesus, may our words be spoken out of love and may we both overlook the small things.*

COULD parishes invite mentor couples to check in on newlyweds at the three-month, six-month, one-year mark?
—Fr. Joseph Healey, MM

Ongoing formation

REFLECTION. There is much preparation that goes into planning the big marriage proposal and even more planning going into the "big day." Only a session or two is given to the sacramental preparation, and we know that is not enough.

How about those newlyweds we all know who are in their first year of marriage? Call them, check on them, and be a support for them.

PRAYER. *Lord God, use our wisdom to help actively support newlyweds.*

E HAVE had our highs and lows, God's grace sustains us as husband, wife, parents and best friends.

JUNE 29

—Michael and Maureen Malloy

A testament to love

REFLECTION. If people were honest we would have to sit and listen a long time to the response to the everyday question; how's it going? We never really know other people's journey or struggle unless we take the time to get to know them.

What makes the difference in the life of a Christian? Loving as God loves through the highs and lows.

PRAYER. *Merciful God, thank You for Your grace which sustains us through life.*

F YOU return evil for good, evil will never depart from your house. —Prov 17:13

JUNE 30

Am I evil?

REFLECTION. God created us in love and because of love and for love: not for evil. Every day we have choices to make and the choice of doing evil is in our hands.

Do we give in to temptation? Are we selfish? Do we ignore the poor? Do we judge others? Do we fail to forgive? In marriage we help each other get to Heaven and assist each other in choosing good.

PRAYER. *Lord, You call us to be holy as You are holy. Help us to grow in love and truth.*

CHRISTIAN who does not take the
dimension of martyrdom seriously in
life does not understand the road that
Jesus has indicated. —Pope Francis

The Cross before me

REFLECTION. There is a great deal of similarity
between following Jesus and being married.
There is an abundance of joy and love in both,
and we can be overwhelmed with emotion
which is beautiful. There is also the Cross.

The road we follow leads to sacrifice, self-emptying, and the Cross. This death also leads to new
life and so we should embrace and love the Cross.

PRAYER. *Loving Father, may we stay the
course in following You and in loving each
other no matter the sacrifice.*

AITH without works is futile.
—Jas 2:20

Less talk, more action

REFLECTION. There are many secular phrases
that mirror the words of St. James. Elvis Presley
had a song with the phrase, "a little less conversation and a little more action."

Whether it's St. James or Elvis, the sentiment
is the same because actions speak louder than
words. Loving words encourage and inspire;
loving actions give power to our words.

PRAYER. *Jesus, thank You for Your words of
love and Your action of love on the Cross.*

EVERYONE should be quick to listen but slow to speak and slow to anger.

—Jas 1:19

JULY 3

Two ears, one mouth

REFLECTION. In God's design He gave us two ears and one mouth. The thought being perhaps that we should listen twice as much as we speak.

Who listens to you? I mean who really listens? For married persons the one who listens best should be our spouse. In listening to the whole person we will communicate their importance to us and our love.

PRAYER. *Heavenly Father, thank You for Your patience in listening to our prayers.*

BE DOERS of the word and not just hearers who only deceive themselves.

—Jas 1:22

JULY 4

Connect the dots

REFLECTION. The Christian who is the faithful servant is not the one who knows the most theology or who has studied in Rome but rather the one who puts God's Word into practice.

You don't need a Ph.D. in Systematic Theology in order to pray with your spouse and kids or to forgive as Jesus has forgiven you. Marriage is the school of love.

PRAYER. *Lord God, may we be open to hearing Your Word and obedient in doing it.*

FOR judgment will be without mercy to the one who has not shown mercy. **JULY 5**

—Jas 2:13

What goes around comes around

REFLECTION. Mercy is very appealing because let's face it, no one wants what we really deserve when we stand before God. Only a fool is unaware of their own faults.

The sins we commit can be forgiven and our response to receiving God's mercy is to be merciful to each other. Every day we will have opportunities to show mercy to our spouse and others.

PRAYER. *Merciful Father, may we be merciful to each other as You are to us.*

YOU can see, then, that a man is justified by works and not by faith alone. **JULY 6**

—Jas 2:24

Our understanding of faith

REFLECTION. When the Gospel writer and Apostle St. John wrote about belief, the word he used was a verb, an action word. Our minds are certainly activated by intellectual pursuits and discussing ideas is important.

For the Christian, faith doesn't end there for what we believe needs to be put into practice. It is by our actions that we will be judged.

PRAYER. *Lord God, may our knowledge of Your Word find expression in our actions.*

I HAVE long since come to believe that people never mean half of what they say and it's best to disregard their talk and judge only their actions. —Dorothy Day

JULY 7

Talk can be cheap

REFLECTION. Dorothy Day was a woman of conviction who lived out her faith on the lower east side of Manhattan serving the poor and abandoned among other service.

Many people talk about praying for the poor but never spend time with them. What areas do you need to improve in as a couple? Plan to serve others together.

PRAYER. *Jesus, at the end of each day may our actions reflect Your words.*

W HAT is the source of these conflicts and quarrels among you? —Jas 4:1

JULY 8

The root of the cause

REFLECTION. St. James and St. Paul spent a great amount of time pleading for unity and peace among the believers of their day. While even those who lived closest to Jesus had conflicts like we do, the question is asked, "What is the source?"

When conflicts arise take time to seek what lies behind the behavior and begin the process of getting it out in the open.

PRAYER. *Jesus Christ, self-examination can be difficult, help us be honest with ourselves and others.*

NDEED, those who had perseverance are the ones we call blessed. —Jas. 5:11

JULY 9

Run the good race, fight the good fight

REFLECTION. Marriage is certainly not a sprint but a long haul, full of potential roadblocks and unforeseen obstacles. This is why faith in God and a sacramental understanding of matrimony is vital to the good health of marriage.

There is no problem greater than God's love, and when the Holy Spirit is active in our marriage we will persevere.

PRAYER. *Lord, when the hardships seem too much for us, surprise us with Your love.*

 R THINK of ships. Even though they are large…they are steered by a very small rudder. —Jas. 3:4

JULY 10

I wish I could take that back

REFLECTION. How many times have we wished we could go back in time, if only a few minutes, and stop those words from coming out of our mouths! Even though they are spoken for only a few seconds they can be remembered for a lifetime.

Be careful what you say but, even better for a healthy marriage, forgive one another from the heart.

PRAYER. *Jesus, forgive us both for the unkind and insensitive things we have said.*

PRAYER after all, is concentration on God. **JULY**
—Blessed Miriam Teresa Demjanovich

11

The couple that prays together…

REFLECTION. It can be difficult for couples to pray together if they have never seen or experienced other couples praying together. If it's not part of your experience before marriage it will be a challenge—but not impossible—to incorporate it into your life.

Make the time daily, morning or night, to pray together. Praying together is the glue of marriage.

PRAYER. *Lord, move in our hearts that together we may concentrate on You.*

DEAR Parents, have great patience, and **JULY**
forgive from the depths of the heart.
—Pope Francis

12

We replicate ourselves in our children

REFLECTION. Many of our physical characteristics appear in our children. "She has her mother's eyes," or "he laughs just like his old man." In the home we pass on life lessons which are more "caught" than "taught."

If we forgive, our children will pick up on it. If we pray…so will our children. Patience and forgiveness and faith will be our legacy.

PRAYER. *Lord, may we live out our faith in joy and pass that on to our children.*

LOVE one another intensely, with all your heart.
—1 Pet 1:22

13

No half measures here!

REFLECTION. Most people have a hobby they make time for or a sports team that they follow throughout the season, and it can provide a healthy outlet and distraction from the routine of life. Some are intense about these interests and they can become "unbalanced."

St. Peter was intense and calls us to be intense with our love of God and each other.

PRAYER. *St. Peter, pray for us for you too were married and understand its demands.*

CONDUCT yourselves honorably.
—1 Pet 2:12

JULY
14

Strength and honor

REFLECTION. You don't read much about honor or valor anymore. The tabloids and social media feeds are filled with behavior that tends to highlight the dishonorable and shameful.

As people of faith we can do better and are in fact called to do better. At the end of the day and at the end of life that which is honorable will be remembered.

PRAYER. *Jesus, help us to bring out the best in each other so we can give honor to You.*

E SHEPHERDS of the flock of God that has been entrusted to your care.

—1 Pet 5:2

JULY 15

These are *my* children

REFLECTION. How many times a day do my wife and I talk about our children? Too many to count and surely our children are the great crown of our marriage.

While they are our children we know that they belong to God, and we are simply entrusted with them for as long as we have breath within us. Thank You God for the gift of children.

PRAYER. *Jesus, allow us to be good shepherds with the children You have entrusted to us.*

 O NOT lord it over those in your charge, but be examples to the flock.

—1 Pet 5:3

JULY 16

Servant leadership

REFLECTION. Managers make you feel that they are important while leaders make you feel important. The same is true in business as it is in the Church or a family.

We all know the boss or coach or priest who is more concerned about themselves than they are with those they are supposed to lead and minister to. Where were you a good "servant" today?

PRAYER. *Lord God, may we humble ourselves as You did and serve our family with Your heart.*

CAST all your anxiety on him, because he cares about you. —1 Pet 5:7

JULY 17

Anchors away!

REFLECTION. Every person needs an outlet to vent the day's problems to or to let off some steam. There are some harmful outlets that can cause more issues than they solve.

As Christians we have God Himself as our biggest advocate who is always willing to hear us. Share your cares with each other and then "cast them on Him" because He cares for you.

PRAYER. *Jesus, hear us now as we cast our cares and concerns on You in prayer.*

MARRIAGE should be honest and open, full of trust and rooted in faith and love.—Dan and Rachel Crum

JULY 18

Solid roots equal a fruitful tree

REFLECTION. The beautiful, fruitful trees and gorgeous flowers we see above ground are the result of a lot of work beneath the soil. This is similar to marriage because it too takes work.

When we observe a happy and healthy marriage we know it doesn't just happen. Good communication, trust, and lots of love and faith go into making a happy marriage and happy home.

PRAYER. *Lord God, may we be united in love as we place our trust in You for all things.*

GREET one another with a loving kiss.
—1 Pet 5:14

JULY
19

Six days on the road

REFLECTION. After a journey away from home there is nothing like returning home to the love a family and spouse can provide. Especially after the daily grind of work, it's nice to be greeted with a hug and a kiss.

Never take those moments for granted and when you hug or kiss each other, make it intentional, make it count.

PRAYER. *Lord God, forgive us for those times when we neglected each other.*

BE DILIGENT in providing a firm foundation for your call and election.
—2 Pet 1:10

JULY
20

Rock solid

REFLECTION. St. Peter is talking about our call to enter into a living relationship with Jesus Christ and our foundation of faith in Jesus and in His word. In marriage that faith foundation is essential.

If it's based on something other than Christ such as outward appearance, social status, or convenience cracks will show up. Make the foundation Jesus.

PRAYER. *Lord, guide us so we are always attentive to our faith which calls us to trust You.*

FOR I think it is right, to refresh your memory as long as I remain in this body.
—2 Pet 1:13

Put your clothes away…and gym bag and dishes

REFLECTION. It's not always what you say but how you say it. St. Peter writes that he will "refresh your memory" in regards to the teaching of Jesus.

In marriage there will be times when your spouse will annoy you and even appear not to hear you. Yes, it happens. At those times, be gentle in speech and remember to respond with love.

PRAYER. *Holy Spirit, remind us both to call on You when we are on the verge of losing it.*

WHEN I pretend that the idea was his he usually is on board with it.
—Sophia and Ronald Weasley

Figuring each other out

REFLECTION. Each married couple has to figure it out along the way. Every one of us is a sinner and as they say, "perfection only in Heaven."

Our spouse is not a puzzle to be solved but a mystery to be loved. There will be times when their behavior will mystify you but after some time you'll figure each other out. Love them along the way.

PRAYER. *Jesus, I don't always understand You or my spouse. Let me love You both along the way.*

THEY will introduce their disruptive views and even deny the very Master who redeemed them. —2 Pet 2:1

United, not divided

REFLECTION. When we plant a tomato plant or other vegetable we take great care to protect it from insects, harsh weather, or animals who will destroy them. Our marriage needs to be protected with even greater vigilance than a plant.

There will be people who will seek to divide you by gossip, placing doubt, and negativity. Weed them out of your marriage.

PRAYER. *Lord, keep us focused on the truth and help us to identify those who divide and disrupt.*

 HOWEVER, the Day of the Lord will come like a thief. —2 Pet 3:10

Judgment day

REFLECTION. St. Peter warned the early Christians to stay faithful to Christ for He is coming again. While we await the second coming of the Lord we know we don't know the day or the hour. Our own day or hour is unknown as well.

We all know people who have died suddenly through accident or disease. Each day is a gift; never take life for granted.

PRAYER. *Mary, Mother of God, pray for us as we live each day to the fullest.*

ROW in the grace and the knowledge of our Lord and Savior Jesus Christ.

—2 Pet 3:18

Grow up in your faith

REFLECTION. For many adults religious education stopped in eighth grade, and if you reflect on your maturity level as an eighth grader it's scary!

While you both have matured and grown physically, emotionally, and professionally, has your faith grown up with you?

PRAYER. *Jesus, help us to pursue quality adult faith formation together.*

———

ROGRESS...consists in persevering attempts, which necessarily imply failures.

—Blessed Miriam Teresa Demjanovich

Move forward, focus ahead

REFLECTION. In any endeavor we undertake there are countless "failures" along the way. Even the most gifted artists and athletes take missteps and suffer setbacks.

In marriage we will have failures as well, at times daily. The key will be to move forward by forgiveness and perseverance. The Holy Spirit is with you both; call out to Him.

PRAYER. *Holy Spirit, our Advocate, assist us in loving each other and moving forward.*

AY mercy, peace, and love be granted you in abundance. —Jude 1:2

A gift to be received

REFLECTION. There are obvious differences between men and women physically, psychologically, and a plethora of other areas. Often men desire to work for everything they have; receiving something as a gift can be awkward.

Christian life for men and women involves the humility to graciously accept the gifts God freely grants us.

PRAYER. *Lord Jesus, may we humbly accept the measure of mercy, peace, and love You grant us.*

 IGHT earnestly for the faith that was once and for all entrusted to the saints. —Jude 1:3

Fight the good fight for faith

REFLECTION. The way that God determined was best to share His love for you and me and all of humanity was not through a billboard or skywriting in the clouds but through personal relationships.

He came to us in Jesus and Jesus sent out the Twelve. This faith is to be handed on first and foremost in the family. Speak of this faith and model it for others.

PRAYER. *Loving Jesus, help us to know the truth and to share the truth You reveal to us.*

HEY are shepherds who feed only themselves. —Jude 1:12

Our true vocation

REFLECTION. St. Jude has some pretty harsh words for those who selfishly choose themselves over others. No matter what vocation we are called to, married, single or religious life, our true vocation is to belong to Christ.

Jesus, our Good Shepherd, guarded and served the sheep entrusted to Him. How are you serving your spouse this week?

PRAYER. *Jesus, impel us to serve You and serve each other intentionally this week.*

T IS these people who create divisions, who follow their own instincts and do not possess the Spirit. —Jude 1:19

A supernatural love

REFLECTION. A good Old Testament definition of a fool is one who follows his own way and relies on self. Marriage is ordained by God and He gives us the Holy Spirit to live out the vows we make.

His grace is enough. His Spirit allows us to live in unity and love as He does. An outward sign of the Holy Spirit is joy, peace, and loving as God loves.

PRAYER. *Our Lady of Good Counsel, pray for us that we may possess the Spirit of God.*

EEP yourselves in the love of God.
—Jude 1:21

Let it out and let it in

REFLECTION. The love of God is available to all, every one of us. In fact, no one is outside the scope of God's love. We learned from Adam in the Garden of Eden that while God never turns His back on us, we can turn our backs on Him.

Make it a point each day as a couple to pray with and for one another and then you will keep yourselves in the love of God.

PRAYER. *Father of mercy, draw us closer and closer into the chambers of Your Sacred Heart.*

DO not understand my own actions, for I do not do what I want.
—Rom 7:15

AUG.
1

A mystery unto ourselves

REFLECTION. Because of original sin we have been wounded in one way or another which causes disharmony in our life. We can revert to destructive habits and behaviors which seem to have control over us.

Admitting that we are powerless to "fix" ourselves is often the first step to recovery. Powerlessness does not mean hopelessness.

PRAYER. *Lord, help us to change the areas of our life that are harmful to our well-being.*

I HAVE the desire to do what is good, but I cannot do what is good. —Rom 7:18

The struggle of the Saints and ourselves

REFLECTION. From Scripture we know that many of God's people—including Saints—had destructive behaviors. We can become slaves to our disordered desires, and we may not even be aware of it.

The Saints and all Christians rely on hope—a way to begin to change which admits our powerlessness and surrenders our control to God.

PRAYER. *Loving Lord, heal us from sin as we surrender to You every aspect of life.*

T HE least power of love is already greater than the greatest power of destruction.
—Cardinal Ratzinger (Pope Benedict XVI)

God is greater still

REFLECTION. While we may be aware of what the right thing to do is, we can choose to disobey and end up hurting ourselves and loved ones. We are not designed to live and love on our own power and God understands that.

When we surrender to Him with our heart and our soul He takes up residence in our hearts and can and will make us whole and holy.

PRAYER. *Lord, increase our love for You and one another trusting in the power of love.*

YOU are my friends if you do what I command you. —Jn 15:14

Faith seeking understanding

REFLECTION. Many people will trust a friend because of past experiences. When they ask us to do something that doesn't make sense is when we put our trust into action.

God desires that same level of friendship with us. Faith is not an intellectual pursuit but involves obeying God's Word even when we may not fully understand it.

PRAYER. *Lord, may our marriage be marked by our friendship with You.*

ABIDE in me, as I abide in you. —Jn 15:4

Come and stay for a while

REFLECTION. The word "abide" appears over twelve times in chapter fifteen of the Gospel of John. The only other time it appears is in John chapter six where Jesus is speaking about the Eucharist.

Abiding or remaining with Jesus is so important for our faith to flourish because it allows us to be united to the One whom we model true love after.

PRAYER. *Mary, Mother of God, be a Mother to us as we seek to stay close to Jesus.*

ET not my will but yours be done.
—Lk 22:42

AUG.
6

Care in the midst of crises

REFLECTION. Jesus gave us the perfect example of surrender to God's will. In the providence of His life He was willing to turn over everything, the good and the bad, the joy and injustice into the loving care of His Father.

It's difficult to put someone else's will ahead of our own, but when we put God's will first we can joyfully serve our spouse.

PRAYER. *Lord, help us seek Your will for us in all things trusting in Your Sacred Heart.*

PEAK Lord, your servant is listening.
—1 Sam 3:10

AUG.
7

God speaks in the silence of the heart

REFLECTION. How often do we adopt the opposite attitude of Samuel and approach God demanding, "Listen Lord, your servant is speaking!" Often we want God to do the listening and be at our beck and call.

In our relationship with God and with our spouse we should consider the example of Samuel who had an attentive heart and listening ears.

PRAYER. *Heavenly Father, may we be disciplined each day to make time to listen.*

LET God work in your life without being consulted by you.

—Blessed Mother Teresa

AUG.
8

Sign the work order

REFLECTION. God wants the best for us all the time. He is a Father Who sees far further into the future than we can. What God desires for us is, well, everything! Because when God loves, His love is all consuming.

When couples give their lives and marriages over to God and give Him free rein in their lives they can experience the joy He intended.

PRAYER. *Jesus, we commit to giving You free rein in our lives. Do as You please.*

WHATEVER comes to us is from him. —Blessed John Henry Newman

AUG.
9

His choice is best

REFLECTION. Some people are optimists and others are pessimists. To the pessimist, even when good things happen they wait for the "other shoe to drop" as if God is looking for opportunities to squelch their joy.

In marriage each spouse may have a different outlook or personality, but both should agree that God desires only the best for them.

PRAYER. *Lord Jesus, help us to accept everything in life as a gift, the good and bad.*

COME to me, all you who are weary and overburdened, and I will give you rest.
—Mt 11:28

Make a decision for Christ

REFLECTION. Much of our lives are given over to the schedules of others. When we get married and have children even more of our life can be out of our control, and we can begin to lead an unexamined life.

Jesus calls us to Himself and we have a clear decision to make. Take time with your spouse to see if God is your steering wheel or spare tire.

PRAYER. *Lord, help us to choose You every day and to trust in Your will for our marriage.*

AN HONEST explanation always has more grace and force to excuse us than a lie. —St. Francis de Sales

Free from fear of conflict

REFLECTION. In marriage as in life there are times when we need to confront others and even our spouse. Fear, the great enemy of love, causes us to flee and avoid confrontation out of our desire to be accepted, to be loved.

For many, confrontation is a cross to bear until they realize that they are loved, plain and simply, for who they are.

PRAYER. *Jesus, stand with me in love as I confront people for their unacceptable behavior.*

TAKE the words "always" and "never" out of your arguments. Those words put walls up before you even have a chance to talk. —Sean and Daniela McDonnell

AUG. 12

But he NEVER listens!

REFLECTION. Arguments in marriage are a given. What separates the healthy marriage from the unhealthy is how we go about resolving our disagreements. Saying things like, "She always nags" or "He never puts things away" only exacerbates the problem.

Ground rules for arguing may differ couple to couple, but it's good to have them in place.

PRAYER. *Lord, help us to get along and to examine the root cause of our arguments.*

TO SIN is human, but to remain in sin is devilish. —St. Catherine of Siena

AUG. 13

Step into the light

REFLECTION. St. Catherine of Siena is a Doctor of the Church which means she has made an outstanding contribution to the understanding of the Scriptures and Christian doctrine.

While the word "devilish" is out of style in today's vernacular, her words remain true. Recognizing our sin is one thing and refusing to change is another. Do you remain in sin?

PRAYER. *Lord, help us to ask forgiveness and to be free from selfish pride.*

O FORCE can prevail with a father like the tears of his child. **AUG. 14**

—Pope Saint Clement I

Confession and contrition

REFLECTION. Admitting our sins is a good first step, but experiencing contrition or heartfelt sorrow is another thing. Both are necessary before God and in marriage as well.

Because we are not perfect, we have to pray for the humility to be moved when we realize we hurt the one we love.

PRAYER. *Merciful Father, may we be sensitive to our faults and forgive from the heart.*

 HE Church is a house with a hundred gates: and no two men enter at exactly the same angle. **AUG. 15**

—G. K. Chesterton

A desire to change

REFLECTION. When confronting negative behavior in ourselves we know that we need to change because the evidence of our bad behavior is very clear. Not only do we get in trouble but it affects our loved ones too.

Knowing we need to change is evident. Having the desire to change is where real growth can begin. In what areas do you need to change?

PRAYER. *Lord, help us to change in the areas we need and to become witnesses of love.*

TRUE humility makes no pretense of being humble. —St. Thomas More

AUG. 16

The "thanks" belongs to God

REFLECTION. There seems to be so much pressure to achieve and to set oneself apart in society in order to let others know that you're valuable, you're important.

When our value comes from God who knit us together in our mother's womb and who gave us life, we can let go of the desire to please everyone and relax in the joy that comes from God alone.

PRAYER. *Lord, may our marriage be pleasing to You. We are grateful for our life together.*

LEAVE your gift there at the altar and first go to be reconciled with your brother. —Mt 5:24

AUG. 17

The long walk home

REFLECTION. My mother once made me walk to a friend's house to apologize to his mother. While the house was a few hundred yards away, it was a very long walk and one I have remembered throughout my life.

What a valuable lesson I learned about forgiveness and taking responsibility for my actions. What walks do you need to make to your spouse and to others?

PRAYER. *Forgiving Father, let us search our hearts and make amends with each other.*

N O ONE heals himself by wounding another. —St. Ambrose

Christ sets the example

REFLECTION. The old saying goes, "I was a people person but people ruined that for me!" What do we do with the hurt we all experience in relationships? What do we do with the guilt we may feel when we hurt the ones we love?

We act like Jesus and forgive. We own up to our part in the brokenness and ask forgiveness.

PRAYER. *Jesus, what You ask is difficult so give us Your Holy Spirit to do Your will.*

 FIRMLY resolve, with the help of thy grace, to sin no more and to avoid the near occasion of sin. —Act of Contrition

Resolve and avoid, a path to peace

REFLECTION. One of the greatest acts of mercy and love we can perform is to forgive one another as Christ has forgiven us. Easy to say; difficult to do.

We are not alone in our desire to be Christlike for the Holy Spirit has been given to us for precisely that reason. Forgiving like Jesus is a divine act for which we need His Spirit to move within us.

PRAYER. *Lord, whatever forgiveness I'm holding back affects me and my marriage. Help us forgive others.*

OW this Lord is the Spirit, and where the Spirit of the Lord is, there is freedom.
—2 Cor 3:17

There's more inside you that you don't show

REFLECTION. In freedom God created us and in freedom God calls us to Himself. When we respond to God's invitation to forgive and let go of our old way of life we begin to see things differently. Nothing new is seen but things are seen anew.

To the extent that we let go of sinful behavior and start to forgive others is the extent that we will experience freedom.

PRAYER. *Loving Father, send Your Spirit to us so we may experience freedom from sin.*

 HEN you never talk to a person, he soon becomes a stranger to you.
—St. Teresa of Avila

Communication breakdown

REFLECTION. When people "drift" from the faith or stop going to Mass a good question to ask them is, "When did you stop praying?" When we stop praying or only have the ability to recite formal prayers our faith withers.

The same is true in marriage for when we cease talking to one another and communicating the lifeline of the relationship weakens.

PRAYER. *Jesus, may our lines of communication always be open with You and each other.*

OTHING is more suspicious in a man who seems holy, than an impatient desire to reform other men. **AUG. 22**

—Thomas Merton

Chasing the wind

REFLECTION. They say that opposites attract and perhaps it's the contrasting qualities that our spouse possesses that attracts us to them. There can be a danger however to think that we can change the other person and mold them into our image of them. That is a recipe for disaster.

Change can be positive but it works best when we begin with ourselves.

PRAYER. *Lord, may we both value and love one another as we grow in holiness.*

 HERE are a few things that you just don't kid about in marriage. **AUG. 23**

—Fr. Junior Flores

But I was just kidding!

REFLECTION. A healthy sense of humor is invaluable for married life and inside jokes can be a source of bonding for a couple. We are created in the image and likeness of God and humor is one of the better parts of being human.

Humor should be uplifting to the spirit and positive. When humor puts someone down or belittles a person we are out of line.

PRAYER. *Loving Father, increase our sense of humor and may we never harm each other.*

T O APPHIA our sister, to Archippus our
fellow soldier, and to the Church that
meets in your house. —Philem 1:2

The house is where it happens

REFLECTION. The word home appears thirty
times in the Gospels and the word house
appears ninety-nine times. So much of Jesus'
healing, teaching, forgiving, and dining took
place not in the Temple but in the home.

The early Christians also gathered in homes
before churches were built for worship. How is
Jesus present in your home?

PRAYER. *Living God, may Your presence per-
meate every inch of our hearts and home.*

I ALWAYS give thanks to God when I
remember you in my prayers. —Philem 1:4

Midnight, the stars and you

REFLECTION. Jesus doesn't tell us when to pray
but he models for all believers how to pray. St.
Paul constantly mentions prayer in his letters to
various communities and to his friend
Philemon.

What a gift and a joy to have a friend remember you in a prayer of thanksgiving. Pray for and
with your spouse daily with a thankful heart.

PRAYER. *Lord Jesus, we thank You for the
friendship and love we share with each other.*

AY please and thank you often for those everyday things. **AUG. 26**

—Sean and Daniela Mc Donnell

Every day is a gift

REFLECTION. When a person suffers a catastrophic loss it can be easy to reflect on how much they took for granted. Ask anyone who has lost a house to a natural disaster and they will tell you how life can change in an instant.

When we lose a person we love, the pain is unspeakable. Say please and thank you with a grateful heart to the people God has placed in your life.

PRAYER. *Lord, thank You for the people You have placed in our life.*

 OUR love has given me much joy and encouragement. **AUG. 27**

—Philem 1:7

Reasons to believe

REFLECTION. Imagine yourself standing before a crowd of people who are hurling insults at you. Pretty frightening. Now imagine the same scene but behind you stands a friend who whispers in your ear, I believe in you; I'm here for you; I love you.

What a difference love and an encouraging word can make in a person's life and in your marriage.

PRAYER. *Holy Spirit, let me be the most encouraging voice my spouse hears.*

WOULD rather appeal to you on the basis of love. **AUG.**
—Philem 1:9

28

Love is the law

REFLECTION. Often we hear people make a claim to the law or to their rights which as citizens we certainly enjoy. There are no laws that govern friendships or relationships other than love.

When in marriage we have a mutual understanding of Christian love that is our only appeal. No coercion, no manipulation, no games...just love.

PRAYER. *Jesus, thank You for showing us what love is by Your life, death, and resurrection.*

 E WAS formerly useless to you, but now he is indeed useful to both you and me. **AUG.**
—Philem 1:11

29

Bad reputation

REFLECTION. We soon realize that when we marry our spouse their family is part of the package too. Extended family can be a source of joy but consternation as well.

We can freely choose our spouse but we can't choose their family so there will most likely be those times when we decide to be charitable in action and attitude toward them and hopefully they will do the same for us.

PRAYER. *Our Father, may our love for You be reflected in our actions towards others.*

ET my heart at rest in Christ.
—Philem 1:20

AUG.
30

When it all comes together

REFLECTION. St. Paul is asking a friend, Philemon, to receive his runaway slave back as a brother in Christ. The social structure of the time allowed slavery for a number of reasons, and you could even sell yourself as a slave to pay off a debt.

The Gospel of Jesus goes beyond human social structures and calls us to a new way of life where love rules.

PRAYER. *Father, may our marriage reflect the law of love as we model Gospel values.*

TRIVE to be one with your beloved, always willing the good of the other, knowing this is impossible without God. —Thomas and Cindy Costello

AUG.
31

A united front in Christ

REFLECTION. Millions of people make New Year's resolutions while only a few follow through on them. Our good intentions wane because of lack of will power, accountability, and for a number of other reasons.

We need the Holy Spirit to live our commitment of marriage with our beloved and to will the good of the other all the days of our life.

PRAYER. *Holy Spirit, advocate for us as we strive to serve each other.*

Y PAST, O Lord, to Your mercy; my present to Your love; my future to Your providence. —St. Padre Pio

Signed, sealed and delivered, I'm yours

REFLECTION. Married life in many ways mirrors the life of faith for we bring to the table our past, present, and future and lay them before our spouse in trust that we will be loved through it all.

When God is an active participant in marriage we lay everything before the Lord and say, "here we are; everything is Yours." Is your everything placed before God?

PRAYER. *Jesus our Hope, may You always be an active participant in our marriage.*

FTER almost 30 years we are still not "finishing each other's sentences." —Thomas and Cindy Costello

Hooray for Hollywood

REFLECTION. Park bench. An elderly couple holding each other's hands. Staring into each other's eyes. Cut! A beautiful scene in a movie perhaps, but not always reality.

While those moments may occur, married couples remain individuals with their unique personalities and natures. What differences do you appreciate most in each other?

PRAYER. *Lord, may our differences complement our marriage as we grow in love.*

E HAS spoken to us through his Son.
—Heb 1:2

His Word speaks heart to heart

REFLECTION. There are many examples throughout Scripture of people trying to contact one another. On occasion they send a messenger, other times they knock at the door, and sometimes they call or cry out in a loud voice.

God's Word continues to call out to people to speak to their heart. How can you be more attuned to God's Son?

PRAYER. *Blessed Mother, guide our hearts toward Jesus to receive His Word.*

E SHOULD pay much closer attention to what we have heard so that we do not drift away. —Heb 2:1

No bounds can ever tempt me from you

REFLECTION. Fires tend to go out if they are not tended to. How many people ignore their faith, ignore God Himself who revealed Himself in Jesus?

Marriages fail because people "drift" apart. How can your marriage and your faith life be more intentional so you don't drift apart?

PRAYER. *Jesus, stir Your Spirit within us to be attentive to You and each other.*

HOWEVER, we do see Jesus.
—Heb 2:9

SEPT.
5

It's not what you know but who you know

REFLECTION. Thanks to the incredible growth in technology in the past fifty years, we can explore far into the galaxies and even discover new solar systems. There is still a great deal that we do not know about the "heavens" and the earth.

We are assured that no matter how far the galaxies extend that Jesus is in control.

PRAYER. *Lord, as we journey together in marriage let our eyes and hearts be fixed on You.*

JESUS likewise shared in the same flesh and blood.
—Heb 2:14

SEPT.
6

The humility of God

REFLECTION. There are many titles for Jesus in the Gospels such as Lord, King of Kings, Good Shepherd, and Prince of Peace among others.

While these exalted titles reflect the majesty of God we are reminded that Jesus is our brother. He was hungry and thirsty, grew weary, and wept like we do. He even went to a wedding and kept the party going.

PRAYER. *Lord, stay with us and help us to move forward joyfully in our marriage.*

OR clearly he did not come to help angels but rather he came to help the descendants of Abraham. —Heb 2:16

There is always hope

REFLECTION. Don't worry, the police...the ambulance...the fire department...is on the way. These words are comforting to those in trouble.

Christians take great comfort in the fact that we too have a constant companion in times of trouble, and He cares for us and wants to help us. Come, Lord Jesus!

PRAYER. *Jesus, come to our aid and to the aid of our family for we need Your help.*

———————

 ECAUSE he himself was tested by suffering, he is able to help those who are tested. — Heb 2:18

Purified by the refiner's fire

REFLECTION. People of faith and atheists alike are all subject to pain, suffering, and trials in life; no one is immune. Our marriages will have times of suffering and we will have to figure a way through it together.

Our faith doesn't shield us from all pain, but Jesus assures us He is present with us. Turn to Him in good times and bad for He is present.

PRAYER. *Lord, may our prayer life together be consistent all the days of our life.*

HAM and cheese omelet, white toast and coffee with my wife at an old diner was our thing.

—Walter Sobchak

A home away from home

REFLECTION. Some of the most memorable moments and events in life are not necessarily the most expensive or well planned. They can be part of our daily routine and quite ordinary.

Looking back over many years of marriage we can see that the times we spent together doing ordinary things were some of the most meaningful because they were done in love.

PRAYER. *Jesus, allow us to see Your hand in the ordinary things of married life.*

———————

HEIR parental love is called to become for the children the visible sign of the very love of God. —*Familiaris Consortio*

SEPT. 10

Where do children see God?

REFLECTION. How do children learn about the love of God? The Church reflected on this question and the answer they arrived at was refreshing yet challenging. The answer is parental love!

In the same way God "pours Himself out" into the person of Jesus, parents are called to "pour themselves out" to each other and their children. What are we modeling?

PRAYER. *Lord, help us model and replicate the love in the Holy Trinity for our children.*

THE builder of the house is more honored than the house itself. —Heb 3:3

Bricks and mortar or flesh and blood

REFLECTION. There seems to be a new television show each week highlighting dream homes. These shows are appealing and deceiving. They lead us to believe that having a beautiful home with ample square footage and modern conveniences equals a happy home.

What type of home life are you building daily in your marriage and with your children?

PRAYER. *Lord, keep us focused on the things that matter in a home: love, forgiveness, and faith.*

_____

ENCOURAGE each other every day. —Heb 3:13

I believe in you!

REFLECTION. To encourage is to support, to have confidence, and to give hope to another. Most people love to hear words of encouragement and the power of just one person encouraging us can be enough to get us through any trial.

You may never be the smartest person in the room but you can be the most encouraging! Make it a point to encourage each other.

PRAYER. *Loving Father, Your Word is encouraging to us. Thank You for believing in us.*

THE word of God is living and active. **SEPT.**
—Heb 4:12
13

Sharper than a double-edged sword

REFLECTION. It can be difficult to explain the Bible and certain passages especially to those with no faith. There are classes that make the Bible more confusing than clear.

The Bible is not primarily a historical book to be studied but a relationship to be revealed with the living God who speaks on every page. Read the Bible together to deepen your relationship.

PRAYER. *Holy Spirit, move within us. May the Word of God speak to our hearts.*

NO WILL, no thought, no desire, save **SEPT.**
His!
—Blessed Miriam Teresa Demjanovich **14**

You're kidding, right?

REFLECTION. The interior life of a follower of Jesus is a constant struggle between our will and the will of God. No one has ever aligned their will completely with God's perfectly except Mary, the Mother of Jesus.

What is important is not perfection but the desire and will to be perfect. When couples share this desire to do His will life begins.

PRAYER. *Holy Spirit, help us to grow in faith and align our will to You.*

ET us then approach the throne of grace with confidence so that we may receive mercy and find grace when we are in need of help. **SEPT. 15**
—Heb 4:16

Run, don't walk

REFLECTION. Through the death and resurrection of Jesus we have access to God! Yes, you and I can approach God's throne to both present our needs to God and receive whatever grace we need to make our life matter.

St. Paul speaks of "us" approaching God's throne and how true is that in marriage where we walk together seeking God's mercy and grace.

PRAYER. *Heavenly Father, be close to us as we come before You to thank You and receive strength for the journey.*

N THE sacraments we discover the strength to think and to act according to the Gospel. **SEPT. 16**
—Pope Francis

Outward sign of God's love

REFLECTION. We long to *hear* words of affection, *see* selfless actions of love, *touch* beauty itself, and *taste* sweetness incarnate. The world comes to us through our senses and God, who created us, wants us to experience His love as we experience each other in and through our bodies.

Sacramental marriage is nourished through the other sacraments.

PRAYER. *Come Holy Spirit, renew our commitment to You and strengthen our marriage.*

HEREFORE, let us leave behind the basic teaching about Christ and advance toward maturity. —Heb 6:1

Grow up or grow old in the faith

REFLECTION. Many people have advanced degrees in business or advanced training in a technical field and pay good money to learn and become an expert in their field.

Unfortunately, many Catholics don't advance in their faith and they continue on with little knowledge of the faith. How are you advancing in your faith? Seek, ask, and knock!

PRAYER. *Jesus, give us a hunger for the truth and lead us to people who can teach us.*

HE world was not worthy of them. —Heb 11:38

Saints are misunderstood by many

REFLECTION. This world with all of its glamour and glitz tends to highlight those who are in the public eye, make millions of dollars, and who make choices that are not virtuous.

The world mocks fidelity, honesty, chastity, and responsibility yet these things Christians hold in high esteem. What's really important to you in your marriage?

PRAYER. *Lord, when the pressures of the world get too much remind us of what's important.*

ET us throw off everything that weighs us down and the sins that so easily distract us. —Heb 12:1

Time to take inventory

REFLECTION. Every professional athlete trains to shed fat and build muscle in order to compete well. We sometimes have to shed negative people in order to live well.

Who or what may be causing your marriage to suffer? Make the hard choices to protect your marriage.

PRAYER. *Jesus, assist us in taking inventory of our life so our marriage may thrive.*

ITH perseverance run the race that lies ahead of us, with our eyes fixed on Jesus. —Heb 12:2

Where are our eyes fixed?

REFLECTION. In the sacrament of marriage we hear the phrase, "Till death do you part." This certainly takes love, forgiveness, and patience for marriage is not a short sprint but rather a long haul.

The advice that St. Paul gives us relates both to faith and marriage. He urges us to persevere when it gets tough and to look to Jesus for help, fix your eyes on Him.

PRAYER. *Lord, there are some days when we feel overwhelmed. Refresh us for the long haul.*

THE one thing I unwaveringly hope for is that he is trying to be a man of virtue. —Janie Jones

What makes a man?

REFLECTION. Hair color, taste in music, athletic, nerdy, intelligent, messy or neat freak? The characteristics we tend to obsess over while we're dating or seeking "Mr. Right" or "Ms. Perfect" don't seem too important to folks who have been married for a long time.

A virtuous person seems to stand the test of time. Are you virtuous?

PRAYER. *Lord, help us to be virtuous and to encourage each other to be our best.*

LET mutual love continue. —Heb 13:1

You're on the right path

REFLECTION. It's good to check in with each other every now and again to see how everything is in the marriage. Like a car going in for a tune up, adjustments need to be made here and there in order for things to run smooth.

Thank God that things are going well and that you can still communicate love with a glance of the eyes and a warm embrace.

PRAYER. *Jesus, we give You thanks for bringing us together and for our many blessings.*

DO NOT succumb to the love of money, but be content with what you have.

—Heb 13:5

**SEPT.
23**

Rejoice in the moment and be at peace

REFLECTION. Money can certainly be a good motivator to people as can other material possessions. But the love of money, the love of comfort and power can ruin people.

Humans can endure almost anything except perpetual prosperity. You don't have much? Thank God and be content. You're worried about the future? In whom do you trust?

PRAYER. *Jesus, You are not Lord at all if You are not Lord of all! We are all in for You.*

IN MATRIMONY and in the family a complex of interpersonal relationships is set up.

—*Familiaris Consortio*

**SEPT.
24**

Navigating the waters of married life

REFLECTION. Marriage and family life are a microcosm of society with the joys and challenges that are involved in each. We don't need a degree in psychology to live in a family although it might not hurt to have one!

What is needed most is love as expressed through patience, understanding, and forgiveness for they can cover the complexities of life.

PRAYER. *Jesus, You lived and grew up in a family. Help us deal with the complexities.*

THE Rosary is my favorite prayer, a marvelous prayer! —Pope St. John Paul II

SEPT.
25

Don't forget your Mother

REFLECTION. For many Catholic couples who get married in the Church praying the Rosary as a family was not part of their experience. They may know what Rosary beads look like and know that there are many "Hail Marys" involved, but if they haven't experienced praying the Rosary they are missing out.

Resolve to pray the Rosary together for one month. Start with one decade.

PRAYER. *Mary, Our Mother, guide us to the heart of Jesus through praying the Rosary together.*

IF YOU can't feed one thousand people, feed one. —Blessed Mother Teresa

SEPT.
26

One day at a time

REFLECTION. Laundry piles never seem to disappear in our house and the sink is usually full of dirty dishes while there is always one more thing to fix or clean. We can allow the mundane tasks of married and family life bury us.

Take time to appreciate the small things, the important things, for the laundry will always be there.

PRAYER. *Lord Jesus, give us the grace to do what we can to run our household well.*

NE must be firm and unchanging with regard to the end but humble and gentle as to the means.

—St. Vincent de Paul

It's not what we do but how we do it

REFLECTION. Parents have to be firm and resolute with their children because as adults they can see further down the road than their children.

Discipline and correction and the occasional punishment is necessary to guide our children so they can be all God calls them to be. In what ways can you be firm but gentle in loving your children?

PRAYER. *Jesus, may we learn from You to correct with gentleness and compassion.*

EOPLE are more impressed by witnesses than by teachers. —Pope Paul VI

The power of a good example

REFLECTION. Rarely do we remember the title and author of our religious formation books, but we almost always remember those who took time for us.

Think of the men and women who cared for us when we were hurting, laughed with us at something silly, remembered us on our birthday. People do remember actions more than words.

PRAYER. *Lord, remind us of the power of a positive witness and thank You for Your love in action for us.*

T IS time for fathers and mothers to return from their exile, because they have self-exiled from the education of their children, and to fully reassume their educational role.
—Pope Francis

Who is educating your children?

REFLECTION. The parents are the first and primary educators of their children. What could be more important than teaching, educating, and just being with your children?

Unfortunately many parents have "farmed out" that role to others and the family, the Church, and society suffer because of it. Who is the primary teacher of your children?

PRAYER. *Jesus, may parents everywhere be the first and primary teachers of their children.*

LOVE for children is the best instructor in their upbringing. Only to one who loves children may they be entrusted.
—Blessed Pauline Von Mallinckrodt

Invaluable treasure

REFLECTION. Two key elements make for a successful teacher: love for the student and passion for the subject. While school teachers can never love like a parent loves, there are many teachers in Catholic and public schools who give sacrificially of themselves in heroic ways.

Be the teacher at home and appreciate the professionals who teach with love.

PRAYER. *Lord God, thank You for the teachers in our life who have imparted wisdom to us.*

LOVE can supply for length of years. Jesus, because He is Eternal, regards not the time but only the love.

OCT.
1

—St. Thérèse of Lisieux

Love alone lasts

REFLECTION. Three weeks after the birth of our first daughter I presented her at the Back to School night where I was teaching. The parents were gracious and everyone remarked, "Before you know it she'll be in high school." She was only three weeks old!

Time goes quickly it's true, so take the time to love each other for it's the only thing that remains.

PRAYER. *Father, let our love be active no matter the length of days we have together.*

AUTHENTIC conjugal love presupposes and requires that a man have profound respect for the equal dignity of his wife.

OCT.
2

—Pope St. John Paul II

Not to rule over but to walk beside

REFLECTION. In 1939 the blockbuster movie "Gone with the Wind" was released. A number of people boycotted the movie because of the famous line Clark Gable spoke to Vivien Leigh on screen; "Frankly my dear, I don't give a damn."

People were shocked that a man would speak to a woman that way. What does your conversation reveal about respect for the opposite sex?

PRAYER. *Lord, forgive us when our speech has not reflected the respect we have for each other.*

POUSES can complement each other, but they can't **complete** each other. Only God can do that.

—John and Lindsay Schlegel

We can't do God's job as much as we may want to

REFLECTION. It's a great joy to be able to give ourselves to our spouse and to have the ability to love them and serve them. While we may even desire to complete them and be their all in all, that's not why we get married and frankly that's not our job, it's God's.

Grow together in Christ and you'll be in a better position to give, serve, and love one another.

PRAYER. *Loving Father, fill us with Your love and may it pour over into our relationship.*

HE Church firmly believes that human life, even if weak and suffering, is always a splendid gift of God's goodness. — *Familiaris Consortio*

From conception to natural death

REFLECTION. It can be said that larger families need greater love because they are called to sacrifice more. Even in small families, however, when one family member is suffering the other members must sacrifice their time and energy to assist the one in need.

What a gift to have opportunities to love and to have love drawn out of us.

PRAYER. *Lord Jesus, give us eyes to see the suffering so we may respond with love.*

Y GOD, I give you this day.
—St. Francis de Sales

Complete control

REFLECTION. Each new day is certainly a gift and like any gift we can take it for granted. Having complete control is an illusion, and as Christians we give everything over to God's will and work as best we can with what we have.

What areas in your married life are you afraid to let go of? Spend time praying and bringing these before God.

PRAYER. *Lord, may we work with the gifts You give us as we trust in Your providence.*

 HERE are you?
—Gen 3:9

His voice continues to call us

REFLECTION. In all relationships it's good to check in with one another to see how each one is doing. Taking care of small problems when they arise can prevent bigger ones. God "checked in" with Adam and asked a simple question which is a relational question.

Where are you in your relationship with God and your spouse? What direction are you moving?

PRAYER. *Almighty God, thank You for reminding us of Your love and calling out to us.*

MY HEART is very heavy with knowing that if I get married, I won't be able to bring a child into the world. I try to trust that God has even bigger and more beautiful plans for me.

—Michelle Duppong

OCT.
7

His plans are better than mine

REFLECTION. Michelle is one of the most faithful and courageous people I know. Hit with the diagnosis of cancer and other health issues at a young age, she has remained steadfast in joy and faith. Through her pain she has been an example of total surrender to and for Jesus.

Where is your faith? Does it depend on good circumstances or feelings?

PRAYER. *Blessed Pier Giorgio Frassati, strengthen us through Michelle's example of unwavering faith.*

 THE Lord lives! Blessed be my Rock! Exalted be God, my Savior! —Ps 18:47

OCT.
8

This one will last a lifetime!

REFLECTION. Many believe that only those who live and die with their sports teams can relate to the thrill of victory and the agony of defeat.

Those who have the gift of faith have the victory at hand for we know the outcome and yes, we win! Even death itself was defeated by Jesus. Cast your cares on Him for He cares for you.

PRAYER. *Jesus, when we are discouraged remind us to fix our eyes on You.*

AY he remember all your sacrifices and accept all your burnt offerings.
—Ps 20:4

Remember when I burned the dinner?

REFLECTION. Married life demands dozens of small sacrifices each day by both spouses in order to make the marriage work. We sacrifice because we love. We put the other before ourselves out of love.

The "burnt sacrifices" of the Old Testament have given way to offering our hearts up to God and serving Him through serving each other.

PRAYER. *Jesus, thank You for remembering our small sacrifices. May we remember Yours.*

 UT I will live for the Lord, and my descendants will serve him. —Ps. 22:31

Formation, formation, formation

REFLECTION. Whatever is important to the parents will be replicated in their children to some degree. How many infants do we see wearing a little baseball, football, or hockey "onesie."

When it comes to passing down the faith, parents play a pivotal role not just in taking their children to church every week, but in their spiritual formation every single day.

PRAYER. *Lord, we accept the responsibility that we promised at our child's baptism.*

THE Lord is my shepherd; there is nothing I shall lack. —Ps. 23:1

OCT.
11

Who is your shepherd?

REFLECTION. Shepherds lead from ahead, encourage from behind, and walk in the midst of the sheep to make sure they are not injured.

We have a Good Shepherd who has become one of us through the Incarnation, and Jesus still leads us, encourages us, and remains with us in the Eucharist. How are you responding to His voice as a married couple?

PRAYER. *Jesus, we listen for Your voice and trust in Your care for us.*

HE MAKES me lie down in green pastures; he leads me to tranquil streams. —Ps.23:2

OCT.
12

We can rest secure with our Good Shepherd

REFLECTION. Sheep will only lie down if they are well fed and feel secure. They should not drink from a stream or "living water" as it's often called in the Bible because their wool will become heavy and they can easily drown.

Thank God that you can be at peace with your spouse and for the ways you both take care of each other every day.

PRAYER. *Lord God, as we follow You we will never fear for our future for it's in Your hands.*

149

E RESTORES my soul, guiding me in paths of righteousness so that his name may be glorified. —Ps. 23:3

We reflect the good things of God

REFLECTION. When you look at my desk at work you'll notice multiple pictures of my children. I am a proud parent like millions of others.

God reveals Himself as a loving father in the Scriptures and like any father He rejoices in His children's successes. He restores us, guides us, and when we look good…He looks good.

PRAYER. *God Our Father, continue to guide and assist us in doing Your will.*

WILL fear no evil, for you are at my side with your rod and staff that comfort me. —Ps 23:4

To protect and guide, not punish

REFLECTION. "Spare the rod, spoil the child." That proverb has been cited in justifying physical abuse and punishment of children down through the ages as if a shepherd 'beats' the sheep he's entrusted with.

Good shepherds use the rod to guide, not beat. How do you guide the children entrusted to you to God?

PRAYER. *Jesus, pour out Your Spirit on us so we may be good parents to our children.*

YOU spread a table for me in the presence of my enemies. —Ps 23:5

Your presence is requested

REFLECTION. Throughout the Old Testament the way to signify peace with God or with neighbor was through a meal. Burnt offerings were split in two and offered to God.

God takes the position of a server, and He sets the table for us. At Mass, God provides the best sacrifice which is His Son.

PRAYER. *Lord, may we model Your example in our service to each other.*

ONLY goodness and kindness will follow me all the days of my life, and I will dwell in the house of the LORD forever and ever. —Ps 23:6

In this house that I call home

REFLECTION. Few things can stir our emotions and memories as the word "home." The Psalmist writes with confidence about dwelling in the house of the LORD forever and ever, and because it's God's house there will be no divisions, no arguments, no fighting, and no tears.

Perfection at last in Heaven. How does your home reflect God's house?

PRAYER. *Christ Our Lord, prepare a place for both of us as we live each day in love.*

I GAVE my heart to Another, just as in marriage spouses commit to each other. Future choices are now exclusive.

—Sr. Mary Joseph Schultz, S.C.C.

OCT. 17

A different call

REFLECTION. What a gift Religious Sisters can be in our lives! The example they give through their commitment to Christ, a life of service, and the vows they make to their community remind us that Jesus is their spouse.

They make a total gift of self to the One who has chosen them and to whom they have said "yes."

PRAYER. *Lord Jesus, help us to commit even more deeply to each other that we may be one.*

 ZÉLIE and Louis Martin are saints because...they evangelized their children through the example of their lives as a couple in the heart of the family.

—Cardinal José Saraiva Martins

OCT. 18

A saintly couple for Christ

REFLECTION. On October 18th, 2015 Pope Francis canonized Louis and Zelie Martin, the parents of St. Thèrése of Lisieux, the Little Flower. The Holy Father asked families to entrust their joys, dreams, and difficulties to them.

This saintly couple knew the joys of parenthood yet also the heartbreak of having four children die at a young age. What a powerful and essential witness faith lived in the home is for our children if they are to live a Christian life.

PRAYER. *St. Louis and St. Zelie, pray for us that we may witness to our faith in the home.*

152

OVE alone counts!
—Blessed Pauline Von Mallinckrodt

What matters at the end of the day?

REFLECTION. It's nice to have all the creature comforts of home and the latest technological gadgets to keep us up to date and occupied.

But ask anyone who hasn't found that special someone to share their life with, raise a family, and be there for them during the peaks and valleys of life, and they'll agree with a 19th Century German Sister: "Love alone counts."

PRAYER. *Mary, Mother of God, reveal to us the Sacred Heart of your Son, Jesus.*

VENING, morning, and noon I will cry out in my distress, and he will hear my voice.
—Ps 55:18

Cry out together

REFLECTION. Life does and will have some stressful moments and they will come to everyone. The challenge of course, is how we deal with the stress.

It's always beneficial for couples to have a healthy outlet they share together to refresh and renew their marriage. As part of your daily "stress release" turn to God as King David did.

PRAYER. *Lord God, it's us again, come to our aid and let us know You are with us.*

THE adage, "never too old to learn" is a great comfort to me.
—Venerable Catherine McAuley

Move it on over

REFLECTION. Venerable Catherine McAuley was the foundress of the Sisters of Mercy, a religious order that was founded to "make real and present" the mercy of God in people's lives.

As the Order grew and new foundations were built she was open to learn all the new things that come along with being in charge. Be open to change and to advice.

PRAYER. *Lord, remind us that there is wisdom that comes to us from You through others.*

WHAT to expect when you're expecting...the unexpected!
—Beatrix Kiddo

From that moment I realized I was a mom...

REFLECTION. One of the most glorious moments for a married couple is when they find out that they're expecting. From the very moment the doctor confirms the news or that "pregnancy indicator" turns the right color, everything changes.

Remember that every life is a gift and in the same way you make room for the baby in your life, make room for God as well.

PRAYER. *Mary, watch over our pregnancy and be a Mother to us and our child.*

ARRIED people too are called to progress unceasingly in their moral life. —*Familiaris Consortio*

You should never stop being a student

REFLECTION. Good teachers have good answers but exceptional teachers ask great questions. The minute we begin to ask a question we become a self-directed student.

While we continually grow and learn in our field of work it's often the case that our religious education stops at about an eighth grade level. Ask questions; seek answers.

PRAYER. *Lord, help us to grow and learn about our faith; lead us to progress in our knowledge of Your will.*

 OW can a young man lead a spotless life? By living according to your word. —Ps 119:9

Give your spouse a pure heart

REFLECTION. The word purity is rarely used these days and those who act in an impure way seem to garnish headlines. There are many challenges to living a pure life, yet it's a virtue worth striving for.

Whatever we allow into our eyes and ears has an effect on our marriage for better or worse.

PRAYER. *Lord, guide my husband by Your Word and together may we serve You with a pure heart.*

EEP me from the way of falsehood, and let me live according to your law.
—Ps 119:29

Desire to do the right thing

REFLECTION. The majority of parents want to do the right thing for their children. That is certainly a "godly" thing to desire. The way they go about it however may not always be from God.

Putting on the mind of God to seek what is best for others is not easy. Keep Christ close through prayer in making decisions.

PRAYER. *Father, may our desire to do the right thing be in line with Your Word and what's best for our family.*

 OUR word is a lamp to my feet and a light to my path.
—Ps 119:105

One step at a time, follow the light

REFLECTION. In marriage we promise to be faithful until death do we part. That kind of commitment is one that is humanly impossible to keep without the help of God to see it through.

Obedience to God's Word will illuminate our actions and conduct toward our spouse. Marriage is a supernatural walk, and we are reminded that God goes with us each step of the way.

PRAYER. *Loving Father, may Your Word be our roadmap as we face each day together.*

AY there be peace within your walls and security in your palaces.
—Ps 122:7

The 'Shalom" that comes from God

REFLECTION. Shalom or peace is a customary Hebrew greeting which also carries the idea of prosperity and interior harmony.

Jesus often says, "Go in peace" after He forgives a person, and it communicates that they are at peace with God and reconnected to the community, too. May God's Shalom be within your home.

PRAYER. *God of Peace, give us Your peace that we may dwell in love and security.*

IFE does not stop and start at your convenience.
—Walter Sobchak

Time and tide wait for no man

REFLECTION. Single people usually can pick up and go at a moment's notice. Few things outside of work responsibilities are present to slow them down. After marriage and when children are part of the picture, we realize that time is not our own.

Appreciate even those inconveniences that life brings because they are part of the big picture and God is in the details.

PRAYER. *Lord, give us patience to be considerate of each other's schedule and to be flexible.*

FOR Christians, marriage, which has its origin in God the Creator, also implies a real vocation.

OCT.
29

—Pontifical Council for the Family

Have you discerned married life?

REFLECTION. Imagine if someone came up to you when you were single and said, "I think God wants you to be a priest or a religious sister." What would your reaction be?

Do we discern the call to married life with the same seriousness that we would discern religious life? Marriage is a vocation with the same dignity as religious life.

PRAYER. *Lord, thank You for the vocation of marriage. May our love reflect Your love for us.*

LOVE seeks one thing only: the good of the one loved. It leaves all the other secondary effects to take care of themselves.

OCT.
30

—Thomas Merton

Love you more

REFLECTION. Never forget the early years when you first fell in love with your spouse. The flirting, the first dates, the laughter, and the sharing should be kept safely in your heart.

Be open to make new memories with your spouse and to treasure those times when it's just the two of you.

PRAYER. *Heavenly Father, with gratitude for all the ways we glimpse Your love in our lives, we thank You.*

HERE is no harder work than marriage, but perhaps nothing that is as rewarding.   —Brad and Kristy Keely

OCT.
31

Give me the ball, coach

REFLECTION. Professional athletes are paid to perform at a high level no matter the circumstances or opposition they face. It's hard work and a long road to the pros but one that's worth the struggle.

Married life also calls for commitment and hard work, but when lived successfully there is nothing better in life.

PRAYER. *Lord, we pray for guidance and for trust when only silence meets our prayers. It's OK for we know You are there.*

F WE really want to love we must learn how to forgive.   —Blessed Mother Teresa

NOV.
1

Go easy, step lightly, stay free

REFLECTION. They say that when you forgive you set a prisoner free and you soon realize that you were the prisoner. Mother Teresa was obedient to Jesus and even when she didn't "feel" His presence she was faithful in following His words.

Who comes to mind when you read about the importance of forgiveness? Forgive them and release the grip they have on you.

PRAYER. *Lord, may we forgive each other from the heart and in humility ask forgiveness.*

FIND someone that makes you laugh, smile, and feel joyful inside and I truly believe that's all you need.

NOV. 2

—Erik and Melissa Gennaro

God put a smile on your face

REFLECTION. One of the things that couples receive before their wedding and as newlyweds is advice. Some advice is solicited and other advice is, well, given anyway.

Happiness can be a sign that God is in the mix and where there is laughter, the Holy Spirit is also close by to make our joy complete. The face will radiate what the heart knows to be true.

PRAYER. *Jesus, increase our joy. May our laughter together be an outward sign of Your love.*

MARRIAGE is more than just loving someone. You have to be committed to working together every day.

NOV. 3

—Shawn and Toni Rejcek

We should be committed...in a good way

REFLECTION. Marriage is not something we should take lightly for it is a lifelong commitment through good times and bad, sickness and health, and through better or worse.

The "work" of marriage will reveal itself in time for each marriage is different because each person is unique. Don't be afraid to commit your energy to make it work.

PRAYER. *Lord, let us work at our marriage and never take love for granted.*

THE family is the heart of the new evangelization.
—Pope St. John Paul II

The original small Christian community

REFLECTION. The phrase, "new evangelization" has been receiving a lot of attention lately as the Catholic Church intensifies her efforts to share the faith with those who don't know Jesus and those who no longer practice the faith.

Parents are the first and primary educators of the faith. There is no greater gift you can give your children than Jesus.

PRAYER. *Lord, may we teach and witness the faith to the children You bless us with.*

THE Eucharist develops the affective love proper to marriage in daily giving to one's spouse and children.
—Pontifical Council for the Family

The gift that keeps on giving

REFLECTION. The "I do" that a couple says during their wedding vows is the first of many "I do's" that they will say to one another throughout their lives.

The most profound gift is the gift of self, body and soul. It's this gift that Jesus gives us each time we celebrate Mass for we hear the words of Jesus, "This is my body, which is given up for you."

PRAYER. *My Lord and my God, may we imitate the One we receive every day in every way.*

ISTENING is a selfless act and an art to do well in marriage. Listen to understand; learn and empathize with each other. —Chris and Terri Apuzzo

The art of listening well

REFLECTION. My great uncle had a primitive hearing aid that he occasionally turned down so he didn't have to listen when he didn't want to.

As appealing as it may be at times to tune our significant other out, it's not recommended for it causes more problems than it solves. Tune in and be attentive for listening communicates love.

PRAYER. *Lord, thank You for not tuning us out when we come before You.*

MARRIAGE is not 50-50, it's 100-100. You each have to give 100% for it to work. —Shawn and Toni Rejcek

No half measures

REFLECTION. So often we hear that marriage is a 50-50 proposition with the idea being that each spouse gives 50%. That mentality leaves each person half filled. It's a supernatural act to give 100%, but that's what marriage demands and draws out of us.

When we have our needs filled by God we will be free to give of ourselves because we are connected to love Himself.

PRAYER. *Come Holy Spirit, let us give all and never hold anything back.*

UR marriage is one of teamwork. **NOV.** From dishes and diapers to big deci- **8** sions and spiritual growth, we work together. —Matthew and Olivia Higgins

True wisdom

REFLECTION. Members of a sports team or medical research committee form a cohesive unit when they are all on the same page and have their goals clearly identified.

We often don't think of marriage this way, and while the analogy isn't perfect it's good to communicate every day and to work together in both the material and spiritual tasks of life.

PRAYER. *Loving Father, remind me to encourage my spouse and to work together in love.*

 IVE something, however small, to the **NOV.** one in need. It's not small to the one **9** who has nothing.
—St. Gregory Nazianzen

Be generous with your words and possessions

REFLECTION. Catholics are called to follow the example of Jesus who was generous with His gifts. When He was hungry Jesus didn't use His gifts to feed Himself but when He saw the hungry crowds He fed them.

It goes the same for our words as well. Are you generous with your praise, encouragement, and reassurance of your spouse? The day is not over yet.

PRAYER. *Jesus, may our words reflect love and appreciation each and every day.*

ARRIAGE is walking through the ups and downs of life with your best friend, with God's help to achieve amazing things.

NOV. 10

—Henry and Mary Hom

Live long and prosper

REFLECTION. Unlike the stoic Dr. Spock of Star Trek fame, the ups and downs of married life can be exhilarating and depressing. We forget that Jesus is with us each step of the way.

Jesus gives us His word that all things can work together for good for those who love Him. We can do better than survive; we can thrive.

PRAYER. *Jesus, open our eyes to the bonanza of blessings that we already have in our lives.*

Y DAD was selfless, soulful, hilarious, quietly observant, and the smartest man I've ever met. His relationship to nature is ever-present within me.

NOV. 11

—Jessica Grygo

A Father's love

REFLECTION. Children are the gift we give to the future. A mother and father complement each other in raising their children and each impart much more than just their DNA.

Do things together with your children even when you can do it faster without them. At every stage of your child's life be their hero and be generous with your time.

PRAYER. *Heavenly Father, thank You for the time we have with our family members.*

ARRIAGES grow when simple things are done together. Eating. Sleeping. Working. Playing. Marriages struggle when these are done alone.

—Alex and Tanya Podchaski

Make room for growth

REFLECTION. While we can't always control outside forces, we can control to some degree what goes on in our family.

Consider eating, sleeping, working around the house, and playing together as the pillars of family life. When these are joined with prayer, our family can become a holy family.

PRAYER. *Lord, help our marriage to be "Holy Ground" where nothing interferes or detracts from family.*

HANK God every day for your spouse and each day choose love in your words and actions.

—Tiernan and John Andrews

Love is a choice

REFLECTION. When we thank God for each other and for the gifts in our life we begin to see life through another lens. Even the inconveniences are viewed differently because God is intimately involved in the details.

Love is a choice that we make every day and how wonderful that we have a new day in order to choose love. Thank You Lord.

PRAYER. *Jesus, help us to choose love as You chose love every day of Your earthly life.*

HAT my dad goes through every day with my mom is both heartbreaking and heartwarming at the same time. Love never fails.

NOV. 14

—Kimberly Tuyp Felter

In sickness and in health

REFLECTION. There is an "app" on the internet that can predict what you will look like in the future. While it may come close to what we may look like there is no "app" that can predict your health status tomorrow let alone 20 years from now.

What a beautiful witness parents give their children in loving through it all.

PRAYER. *Merciful Father, increase our love for one another no matter what comes our way.*

HE light shines in the darkness, and the darkness has not been able to overcome it.

NOV. 15

—Jn 1:5

No darkness too great for God

REFLECTION. Light in the Scriptures often represents the presence of God. Jesus, the Light of the world, calls us to be the "Light of the world," the presence of God.

Married couples frequently light a "unity candle" during the wedding liturgy which is a beautiful representation of Christ's presence in their lives that no darkness can overcome.

PRAYER. *Come Holy Spirit, stir the fire of Your love and light within us.*

ND the Word became flesh and dwelt among us. —Jn 1:14

Love incarnate, made flesh

REFLECTION. Love longs to be expressed. The agony of unexpressed love can even cause physical illness. The vehicle for that expression may be words, actions, or the written word.

God so loves the world that He longed to express His love for each of us in the person of Jesus, the Living Word of God. Take time to contemplate God's love for you.

PRAYER. *Jesus, may our love for You and each other be generously expressed.*

T'S not worth arguing over the small things. Just keep the toilet seat down and move on. —Scott and Danielle Taylor

Choose your battles

REFLECTION. When you first started dating there were those little things that you just loved about the other person and you couldn't wait to tell your friends how special he/she is.

After you tie the knot those cute little things give way to some, well, annoying things. You don't love your spouse any less but it's just the time to practice the art of making marriage work.

PRAYER. *Lord, at the end of the day we are thankful for each other and for Your love.*

UR doctor told us our baby had Downs Syndrome. We said, "He's God's perfect gift to us." The doctor replied, "Wonderful, I'm glad lots of love awaits him."

NOV. 18

—Anna and Simeon Temple

Love is always sound advice

REFLECTION. Our mental image of life with children rarely reflects reality. Life is full of surprises. At these times we stop to wonder why God chose us to be so blessed.

How great is God who does everything out of love and has the perfect child whom He entrusts to our care.

PRAYER. *Blessed Virgin Mary, you always give us a mother's care and for that we are grateful.*

———

 T. JOHN Paul II's "Theology of the Body," has been a source of great joy in our marriage. The lifegiving love that is written into our very being gives us a taste of Heaven.

NOV. 19

—Trish and Jordan Matchen

Male and female He created them

REFLECTION. Men and women both have eyes and tend to see life through different and complimentary viewpoints.

Through active communication and reflection on the Church's teaching on human sexuality we can enjoy the same view of our married vocation. It's a view which values the dignity of each person created in His image and likeness.

PRAYER. *Jesus, help us to be all that You created us to be and to value one another.*

HE MUST increase; I must decrease.
—Jn 3:30

NOV.
20

In faith and in marriage

REFLECTION. The above words were spoken by St. John the Baptist, but in reality they are the words that must be said by every Christian. "I" or our "ego" must decrease and God must increase in our lives.

If we first say "yes" to God and allow Him to work through us we will be better equipped to continue to die to ourselves in order to live for God and our spouse.

PRAYER. *Jesus, what You ask is difficult but with Your grace we will follow Your will.*

JESUS said to her, "I am he, the one who is speaking to you."
—Jn 4:26

NOV.
21

That's the man I'm looking for

REFLECTION. I once gave a presentation and afterwards an older man raved about my talk. I appreciated his kindness, but the next time we met he didn't have a clue who I was. After my presentation he told me that his eyesight was poor so he recognized my voice rather than my face.

Are you attuned to Jesus' voice in your marriage?

PRAYER. *Mary, Mother of God, may we be attuned to the voice of your Son.*

TO MAKE marriage work, spouses must strive to grow closer to God and to each other each day.

—Jeff and Maria Morrow

Every day is an opportunity for growth

REFLECTION. Few people notice the choir in Church unless it's really bad. We tend to take for granted good music, good liturgy, and good marriages when we experience them, but the truth is they just don't "happen." There is a person or team behind the scenes making it work.

Strive for holiness with both God and your spouse.

PRAYER. *Lord, may we grow closer to You together as we strive for holiness as a family.*

YOU know you've done well when you fall in love with your spouse every day of your life.—Michael and Jessica Gromek

Nothing can ever tempt me from she

REFLECTION. Police officers are trained in such a way that they are prepared to expect the unexpected. What may seem routine to some will be viewed slightly different by those who have "seen it all."

In marriage, what a blessing it is to have some consistency in your life. Whether a good day or bad, someone at home is crazy about you.

PRAYER. *St. Michael the Archangel, protect those who protect us as we serve each other.*

THIS man is truly the savior of the world. —Jn 4:42

NOV. 24

Who is *your* savior?

REFLECTION. In the time of Christ the Romans had erected a statue of Caesar Augustus which could be seen by those who were entering the port of Caesarea. It read, "Savior of the world."

The woman Jesus encountered at the well knew that Jesus was and is the true Savior of the world. Is He yours?

PRAYER. *Jesus, save us from the temptation of being our own savior as we trust You for all things.*

LIFE'S challenges should be faced with a smile; besides, you already succeeded if you love unconditionally and keep your faith. —Caitlin Feeley

NOV. 25

Challenges draw love out of us

REFLECTION. To face life's challenges with a smile is easier said than done. There are many variables that are out of our hands and we know the difficulty in trying to change circumstances and people.

Knowing that we face these challenges together and assured of God's love for us allows us to move forward in confidence and joy.

PRAYER. *Lord Jesus, be with us as we face trials and assure us of Your steadfast love.*

171

THEREFORE, what God has joined together, let no one separate.

—Mk 10:9

Indissolubility

REFLECTION. The covenant that husband and wife enter through a valid marriage reflects and makes real the covenant love between God and His people.

It's an outward sign of God's love and fidelity which needs the sacramental life of grace found in the Church to be lived to the fullest.

PRAYER. *Jesus, send forth Your Holy Spirit to strengthen the bonds of our marriage.*

WE LEAVE others free to embrace the Gospel. We do so with the conviction that the truth is what sets us free.

—Bishop Arthur J. Serratelli

We propose the Gospel and never impose it

REFLECTION. Christians have a firm belief that you shouldn't force someone to believe the Good News of Jesus Christ. Belief can't be coerced nor should it be.

That doesn't mean we keep this Good News to ourselves, but rather we share who Jesus is in freedom and joy. If you had three minutes to share your encounter with Jesus, what would you say?

PRAYER. *Holy Spirit, may we be a couple for Christ in how we share our faith in joy.*

O YOU want to get well? —Jn 5:6 **NOV.**
28

What is your pool?

REFLECTION. Jesus approached a man who had been sick for 38 years and sought healing through a pool. The only thing that has changed for most people is where they seek healing.

What is your pool? What do you think will bring life, joy, and healing? When couples are united in Christ and seek His will and obey His Word we experience joy.

PRAYER. *Lord, may our married life together be filled with Your Love, for Your love is enough.*

HAVE come that they may have life, and **NOV.**
have it in abundance. —Jn 10:10 **29**

A lust for life

REFLECTION. We are created for more in this life and the life beyond. We all experience that loneliness, that desire for something more that we just can't put our finger on.

The "world" offers us enticements, gadgets, and other things which while not evil in and of themselves fail to satiate our deepest longings. Turn to Jesus together; trust and you will see.

PRAYER. *Merciful Father, help us to experience the fullness of life which we are created for.*

Y SHEEP listen to my voice. I know them and they follow me. —Jn 10:27

Sheep just need to be reminded

REFLECTION. A shepherd once remarked that sheep are not senseless but they just need to be reminded of where they are going and of who is leading them. God's people are often characterized tenderly as sheep in Scripture.

How are you listening to Jesus and following Him in your marriage? What do you need to be reminded of?

PRAYER. *Jesus our Good Shepherd, make Your voice loud and clear and remind us to follow You.*

 OUR spouse may snore. Sleeping together may not always be the best option. Nothing wrong with sleeping apart so both of you get enough rest.
—Peter and Cristin Durkin

The sweet sound of silence

REFLECTION. Ah, the sweet reality of married life. At one point you really want to sleep with your spouse and then a few years later well, kids in the bed, snoring, tossing and turning.

There will be times when sacrifices will be made for the benefit of each other and the family that will keep you sane. Love seeks the good of the other.

PRAYER. *St. Joseph, watch over us as we sleep and keep us safe and at peace.*

WHOEVER feeds upon my flesh and drinks my blood has eternal life and I will raise him up on the last day.

—Jn 6:54

Your soul is starving

REFLECTION. Jesus is truly present in the Eucharist. Body, blood, soul, and divinity. Is that crazy to believe? Perhaps, but it's nonetheless true. Not because I say it but because Jesus said it over and over on multiple occasions.

If we desire communion with God the same way we want communion with our spouse, then receive the Eucharist.

PRAYER. *Holy Lord, may we receive You humbly and faithfully in the Eucharist.*

YOU know you have a strong marriage when the worst day with your spouse is still better than the best day without them.

—Michael and Kathy Butchko

A student of history

REFLECTION. What a blessing it is to be able to look back through the years, reflecting on the peaks and valleys of married life and come to the conclusion that the worst day with them is still better than the best day without them.

Grow together in faith and thank God that He goes with you each step of the way.

PRAYER. *Abba, Father, help our marriage to be as strong as Your love for us.*

AISING children brings both challenges and blessings, and sometimes the challenges are blessings.

DEC.
4

—Jeff and Maria Morrow

Growing in wisdom and stature

REFLECTION. In the Gospels we read that Jesus grew in "wisdom and in age and in grace." Perhaps parents are the ones who grow in all these areas when they have children.

While growing in age comes naturally, growing in wisdom and in grace doesn't happen all at once for it's a process. When your children drive you nuts, it's an opportunity for growth.

PRAYER. *Mary and St. Joseph, guide us and pray for us when our children drive us crazy.*

F YOU realize that your spouse is upset with you for any reason, stop whatever you are doing and resolve the issue as soon as possible. Talk about it.

DEC.
5

—Marge and Deacon Tom Gibbons

Leave your gift at the altar...

REFLECTION. Jesus was crystal clear about reconciling with your neighbor before going off to worship God. Our spouse is our closest neighbor and in reality "another self."

How will you know that your spouse is upset with you? 99.9% of the time you'll just know. Sweeping things under the carpet will increase disharmony so stop, listen, and talk.

PRAYER. *Lord, may we both value open communication in all aspects of our lives.*

HOEVER abides in me, and I in him, will bear much fruit. Apart from me you can do nothing.

DEC. 6

—Jn 15:5

Should I stay or should I go?

REFLECTION. Abiding or remaining with is not held in high esteem anymore. It's not unusual for people to work for a handful of companies throughout their career, and athletes rarely stay with one team anymore.

Jesus doesn't call us to abide with our place of employment, but He does call us to abide with Himself. How are you staying close to Christ?

PRAYER. *Jesus, we need Your help daily in abiding with You. Help us stay close to You.*

 AINTS and committed Christians are like a window. They allow the light of Christ, His grace and truth, to enter their world to cheer and enliven it.

DEC. 7

—Msgr. James Turro

A window or a door?

REFLECTION. Light comes naturally to both a door and a window yet only the window allows the light through. Likewise, we are called to be as transparent as a window in order to let the light of Christ shine through us.

Are their areas in your married life that could use the light of Christ? Are there any areas closed out to Him?

PRAYER. *Lord Jesus, may our marriage be a window to Your goodness and love for others.*

MARRYING your best friend, being a good listener, and mutual respect are a recipe for a lasting and happy marriage. —Marge and Deacon Tom Gibbons

I saw the light

REFLECTION. Legend has it that the folds in a chef's hat represent the number of ways a chef knew how to cook an egg. The vaunted 100-fold hat is reserved for the heads of only the most knowledgeable culinary experts.

Marriages also have many and varied ways to make them work but the basics of friendship, listening, and respect go into every one.

PRAYER. *Father, without the extras we can do, but without You we won't make it through.*

KNEW my dad was still watching as I rode the bike. I knew he taught me well and I could keep going when he let go. I miss not having him right beside me anymore. —Fr. Jim Chern

Taking the training wheels off

REFLECTION. Memories of our parents tend to stay with us and continue to mold us. One moment they're holding on and then they slowly begin to let go of their physical hold both literally and figuratively.

While their physical grip may lessen, their love never diminishes and extends beyond death itself. What memory are you most grateful for?

PRAYER. *Jesus, may the positive memories of our childhood help form our own children.*

O NOT let your hearts be troubled. You place your trust in God. Trust also in me.

—Jn 14:1

DEC. 10

Double down on trust

REFLECTION. It's easy to rely on yourself when things are going well. What Jesus calls for is to rely on Him and to trust Him. When we trust Him in good times it will be quite natural and easy to trust Him in hard times.

Is the foundation of your marriage built on trust in God or reliance on self? Is prayer and trust in Jesus an act of trust or desperation?

PRAYER. *Lord, into Your hands we entrust our whole life. Jesus, we trust in You.*

AM the way, the truth, and the life. No one comes to the Father except through me.

—Jn 14:6

DEC. 11

Different paths to the Way

REFLECTION. There are not "many" paths to God. There is only one way and that way is Jesus Christ. Different paths may lead to Jesus, but our faith and the Scriptures are clear that Jesus is the way, the truth, and the life.

Jesus is the only Son of the Father who was put to death on a Cross in order to save us from eternal destruction. Are you following the Way together?

PRAYER. *Lord, it can be difficult to always agree in marriage so help us be firm in faith.*

179

MEN, Amen, I say to you, the one who believes in me will also do the works that I do. —Jn 14:12

And do greater things as well

REFLECTION. Marriage is a beautiful setting to do the works of Jesus. Forgiving one another, serving one another, praying with each other, and the list can go on and on.

The word used by St. John for believe is a verb so belief is not just an intellectual pursuit, but rather it's lived out in the providence of daily life.

PRAYER. *Hail Mary, may our hearts and hands reflect our desire to do the works of your Son.*

LWAYS communicate to cooperate. Often anticipate to be able to integrate. Seldom pontificate so not as to separate. Never manipulate in an effort to recreate. —Mary Kominsky

Exhilarate, invigorate, don't obliterate

REFLECTION. When seeking to be successful in any state of life, you should examine the lives of successful people. While your situation will not mirror their's exactly, there are similarities.

Who are the successfully married people in your life? Do you desire a better marriage? Ask questions, observe behavior, and listen.

PRAYER. *Loving God, help support our marriage with other healthy married couples.*

S A young Catholic couple we strive to entrust our marriage daily to the grace received through the sacraments. Then we wake up and try it again.

DEC. 14

—Trevor and Mary Jean Jones

Saying "Yes" to God is a daily event

REFLECTION. Saying "I do" during our marriage ceremony is a once in a lifetime moment...or is it? The first "I do" we say in the church is a cause for celebration, but there is the daily "I do" that is equally important but gets little fanfare.

We can say, "I do" with the help of God's grace charitably poured out in the sacraments.

PRAYER. *Loving Father, give us the daily grace to say, "I do."*

 VERY promise He kept to me throughout my life, I recognized in the writing. And I fell in love.

DEC. 15

—Meghan Brulé

C'est l'amour

REFLECTION. Most phrases sound better in French. There's just something about the language that's appealing to the ear. What is it? *Je ne sais pas.*

While language and dialects differ throughout the country and world, God's voice is the original language of love. It continues to speak *coeur à coeur*, or heart to heart. Allow God to speak to your heart.

PRAYER. *Lord Jesus, open our eyes, ears, and heart as we open the Bible to hear Your Word.*

I T'S for you, Jesus. If you want it, I want it, too. **DEC.**
—Blessed Chiara Badano

16

Live this life well

REFLECTION. Blessed Chiara Badano was a young woman who died from a rare form of cancer at age 18. Despite her poor prognosis, her faith never wavered nor did her joy which came from knowing Jesus.

United in prayer, married couples can say with the same certainty and faith as Blessed Chiara that if Jesus desires it, we desire it too.

PRAYER. *Jesus, may our faith be as strong as the Saints who entrusted all to Your love.*

A M I prepared to entrust to God all that I have? **DEC.**
—Pope Francis

17

How about 70/30?

REFLECTION. God basically just wants one thing from us and that's...everything! Yes, everything. Our faith life is not too different from our married life in that we hold nothing back when we make our wedding vows.

Our human nature does hold back because of fear and sin. Give yourself totally to God, and you'll be free to give yourself to your spouse.

PRAYER. *Loving Father, be patient with us and never let us fear giving everything to You.*

VEN when they share values and interests, men and women don't think in the same way. This is a good thing!

DEC.
18

—John and Lindsay Schlegel

Double vision

REFLECTION. In marriage a man and woman become one flesh but they still retain separate brains, ears, and eyes. This can be a source of conflict if not viewed through the eyes of love.

Even when love abounds we may still be at loggerheads in coming to an agreement when an important decision needs to be made. Listen and pray together.

PRAYER. *Jesus, guide us as we approach life from two different viewpoints united in You.*

 ROM the moment of the Annunciation and conception, from the moment of his birth...Mary followed Jesus step by step in her maternal pilgrimage of faith.

DEC.
19

—Redemptoris Mater

Mary, Mother and disciple

REFLECTION. Many people share in what is called reflective greatness. They are associated with someone famous such as the parents, siblings, or teacher of someone notable.

Mary however, stands on her own two feet and is honored by Jesus for her own faith. How will your marriage be a pilgrimage and witness to faith?

PRAYER. *Hail Mary, may we follow your example of following your Son, Jesus.*

183

Y DAUGHTER Meghan challenges me in ways I was never prepared for. She makes me more intensely aware, and she inspires me along the way.

DEC. 20

—Trish Brule

Children draw out love each step of their journey and ours

REFLECTION. We may be surprised what comes out of our child's mouth when they are little, and it can be a moment of great wonder.

Parenting never ceases and nurturing your child along life's way will provide ample opportunities for continued wonder at what God is doing in their lives and yours too!

PRAYER. *Jesus, may I be open to Your guiding hand in my child's life.*

 NOW that when you are married God will speak to you through your spouse.

DEC. 21

—Justin and Delphine Anderson

La voix de Dieu

REFLECTION. At times we may desire God to speak to us through miraculous signs and wonders. He does speak loud and clear and our spouse can be His mouthpiece.

Moses was saved by four women: his mother, sister, Pharaoh's daughter, and Zipporah, his wife. Never discount the wisdom and guidance of your spouse for they love you and want the best for you.

PRAYER. *Loving Father, let us be attentive to Your voice and to the loving voice of our spouse.*

NURTURE your love and relationship as you raise children; someday it will just be the two of you again.

DEC. 22

—Meredith and Rob Carpenter

Take the long view of life

REFLECTION. Raising children is time consuming and takes a great deal of mental and emotional energy. Most parents are exhausted at the end of the day.

When you take time for each other you will be modeling for your children how healthy couples have healthy, sustainable relationships. Love and nurture your kids and each other.

PRAYER. *Lord, remind us that having time for ourselves is a gift we give our children and each other.*

 I**T'S** one thing to love your spouse; it's another thing to like them. Your spouse should always be your best friend.

DEC. 23

—Brian and Eni Honsberger

I love you...and like you too!

REFLECTION. Jesus calls us to love everyone, even our enemies and that's accomplished by an act of our will. In marriage, as in any working relationship, liking another person is not always easy for we all have little idiosyncrasies that can get on each other's nerves.

Don't let those little things detract from your relationship. Take the time to affirm one another.

PRAYER. *Father, as we rejoice and delight in You, may we delight in each other's friendship.*

JOSEPH, son of David, do not be afraid to take Mary your wife into your home.

—Mt 1:20

DEC. 24

Righteous and obedient to God

REFLECTION. St. Joseph is a man without words but not without witness. What scripture reveals about him is inspiring.

He was righteous, obedient to the voice of God, showed protective love to his wife and unborn child, and assisted in Jesus growing in "age and wisdom." Which of these qualities can you further develop as a married couple?

PRAYER. *St. Joseph, may your example of silent witness inspire us to follow in Your footsteps.*

———————

 THE child is the image of God in the world. —Blessed Mother Teresa

DEC. 25

Merry Christmas!

REFLECTION. The first Christmas spent together as a married couple is usually very memorable as it is the first of many anticipated Christmases together. As others follow and the family grows, the celebration multiplies as well.

Take time as a couple or as a family to fix your gaze on the manger, on Christ. All your prayers are answered within.

PRAYER. *Mary, St. Joseph, be our guides in adoring and loving your Son, our Lord, Jesus.*

E NEED to extend our outreach to those who do not know the Lord.
—Bishop Arthur J. Serratelli

DEC.
26

From our house to yours

REFLECTION. For too long Catholics have followed the mantra of "Pray, Pay, and Obey." Not that these alone are bad things but so much more is needed.

The Church is calling families to share the faith which takes root in the home. The faith founded on Jesus which bears fruit in love, joy, peace, kindness, forgiveness, and sacrifice.

PRAYER. *Lord Jesus, send Your Holy Spirit who compels us to live and share the faith.*

OU can't give God deadlines.
—St. Padre Pio

DEC.
27

All things in His time

REFLECTION. Patience is truly a quality that God builds up in people who believe in Him. The fact that God exists can be found in natural reason and through divine revelation but more often than not what will confound us is His timing.

As we reflect on the birth of Jesus on this day after Christmas we can be assured that God does care and His timing is perfect.

PRAYER. *Lord Jesus, increase our faith as we patiently remain faithful to You in all things.*

THE nearer one gets to God, the simpler one becomes. —St. Thérèse of Lisieux

The view from Heaven

REFLECTION. Married couples should assist each other and their children in getting to Heaven. Of the thousands of decisions and choices we'll make in our lifetime they will be easier to decide when we put God first in our lives and in our marriage.

Choose God every day and as you grow closer to God together life will become simpler.

PRAYER. *Heavenly Father, send Your Holy Spirit to guide our steps closer to You.*

THE loveliest masterpiece of the heart of God is the heart of a mother.
—St. Thérèse of Lisieux

Mary placed Jesus in a manger

REFLECTION. The word "manger" appears once in the Old Testament, in the book of Isaiah, and it's mentioned to shame those who were unfaithful for even a donkey knows its master's manger.

Mary places Jesus in a manger, a place of feeding and a place of nourishment. Jesus, our bread of life, still wishes to nourish us and Mary leads the way.

PRAYER. *Lord, may our hearts be united to the Sacred Hearts of Jesus and Mary.*

YOU have been told what the Lord requires of you: Only to do justice and to love goodness, and to walk humbly with your God.

DEC. 30

—Mic 6:8

Small actions with great love

REFLECTION. St. Francis de Sales remarked that, "Great occasions for serving God come seldom, but little ones surround us daily." Married life has ample opportunities for justice, goodness, and humbly walking with God together.

These are in fact "great things" that the world needs to witness through your marriage. Thank you for your witness of love.

PRAYER. *Loving God, strengthen our marriage as we walk humbly together towards You.*

IN THE chaos of raising a young family, to the quietness of an empty nest, the two shall remain one. Your spouse is your path to holiness.

DEC. 31

—Amber and Nick Dolle

"Gig 'em"

REFLECTION. P.L. "Pinkie" Downs, Texas A&M Class of 1906, coined the phrase "Gig 'em" when at a "Yell Practice" before a college football game. It has become the universal call of encouragement for "Aggies" ever since.

Married couples need to encourage each other with even greater enthusiasm and commitment for the end goal is not a touchdown but Heaven.

PRAYER. *Lord Jesus, may Your Word spur us onward towards Heaven.*

Blessing of an Engaged Couple

HEAVENLY Father,
we praise You for Your wisdom
in arranging that man should not be alone
but should unite himself to another
to form a living cell or unit,
bringing forth new members for Your Kingdom
(Mt 19:5f).
Bless this Couple who have manifested their
intention
to unite in marriage in the future.
Keep them close to You and to one another,
deepen their spirit of prayer and love,
and lead them to receive the Sacrament of
Marriage
with joy and happiness.
We ask this in the Name of Jesus the Lord.

Prayer of Spouses for One Another

LORD Jesus Christ,
help us to love each other
as You love Your Immaculate Bride, the Church.
Bestow on us Christian forebearance and patience
in bearing each other's shortcomings.
Let no misunderstanding disturb the harmony
that is the foundation of mutual help
in the many and various hardships of life.
Inspire us to lead truly Christian lives
and cooperate with the Sacramental grace given us
on our wedding day.
Give us the grace to live together in peace and happiness,
slow to speak harshly
and quick to forgive each other.

Enable us to rear our children in Your love,
assist our neighbor after Your example,
shoulder our rightful civic and religious burdens
in union with You,
and bear witness to You before our community.

Prayer of Spouses
on a Wedding Anniversary

HEAVENLY Father,
we thank You from the bottom of our hearts
for Your continued blessings on our union
that have enabled us to reach another anniversary.
We thank You for letting our love deepen
and for helping us in time of trial.
We know that without Your assistance
we would never have remained so close as we are.
We ask You to continue to watch over us,
over our homes and families.
Help us to renew our vows of love and loyalty
and to strive to remain united with You,
steadfast in our faith and in Your service.

Prayer of Parents for Their Children

HEAVENLY Creator of the universe,
we thank You for the children
that You have entrusted to us.
We want to cooperate with You fully
in helping them grow into free and responsible
persons
and mature in the Faith received at Baptism.
Grant us the grace to be able to guide them
in the practice of virtue
and the way of Your commandments—
by the good example of our lives

and by the loving observance of Your law
and that of Your Church.
Most of all, however, guide them with Your Spirit
so that they may know the vocation You will for
them
and be open to genuine self-giving and true
Christian love.

Prayer for a Family

JESUS, our most loving Redeemer,
You came to enlighten the world
with Your teaching and example.
You willed to spend the greater part of Your life
in humble obedience to Mary and Joseph
in the poor home of Nazareth.
In this way You sanctified that family,
which was to be an example for all Christian
families.
Graciously accept our family,
which we dedicate and consecrate to You this
day.
Be pleased to protect, guard, and keep it
in holy fear, in peace,
and in the harmony of Christian charity.
By conforming ourselves to the Divine model
of Your family,
may we all attain to eternal happiness.

OTHER OUTSTANDING CATHOLIC BOOKS

INTRODUCTION TO A DEVOUT LIFE—Adapted by Sr. Halcon J. Fisk. St. Francis de Sales reached out to everyone through this small book, showing that devotion is available to everyone in every walk of life and occupation. **No. 163**

DAY BY DAY WITH ST. JOSEPH—By Msgr. Joseph Champlin and Msgr. Ken Lasch. Pray with St. Joseph every day with a Scripture verse, short reflection, and prayer. **No. 162**

DAILY MEDITATIONS ON GOD'S LOVE—By Marci Alborghetti. These Scripture verses, brief meditations, and prayers for each day of the year are all focused on God's love for us and praying with them every day will help us to make the sometimes difficult decision to love. 192 pages. **No. 183**

WORDS OF COMFORT FOR EVERY DAY—By Rev. Joseph T. Sullivan. Short meditation for every day, including a Scripture text and a meditative prayer to God the Father. Printed in two colors. 192 pages. **No. 186**

MARY DAY BY DAY—Introduction by Rev. Charles G. Fehrenbach, C.SS.R. Minute meditations for every day of the year, including a Scripture passage, a quotation from the Saints, and a concluding prayer. Printed in two colors with over 300 illustrations. **No. 180**

UPLIFTING THOUGHTS FOR EVERY DAY—By Rev. John Catoir. We can eliminate negative thinking and improve our emotional life by filling our mind with uplifting thoughts. 192 pages. **No. 197**

BIBLE DAY BY DAY—By Rev. John C. Kersten, S.V.D. Minute Bible meditations for every day, including a short Scripture text and brief reflection. Printed in two colors with 300 illustrations. **No. 150**

LIVING WISDOM FOR EVERY DAY—By Rev. Bennet Kelley, C.P. Choice texts from St. Paul of the Cross, one of the true masters of spirituality, and a prayer for each day. **No. 182**

MINUTE MEDITATIONS FOR EACH DAY—By Rev. Bede Naegele, O.C.D. This very attractive book offers a short Scripture text, a practical reflection, and a meaningful prayer for each day of the year. **No. 190**

catholicbookpublishing.com

See more

titles now.

ISBN 978-1-941243-50-3

90000